BLACKSTONE®
GRIDDLING

The Ultimate Guide to Show-Stopping Recipes
on Your Outdoor Gas Griddle

BLACKSTONE® GRIDDLING

JOSH HUNT

Creator of Josh Hunt Griddlin'

PAGE STREET
PUBLISHING CO.

PAGE STREET
PUBLISHING CO.

First published in 2023 by
Page Street Publishing Co.
27 Congress Street, Suite 1511
Salem, MA 01970
www.pagestreetpublishing.com

Distributed by Macmillan, sales in Canada by The Canadian Manda Group.

28   27   26   25   24   4   5   6

ISBN-13: 978-1-64567-991-2
ISBN-10: 1-64567-991-8

Library of Congress Control Number: 2022946836

Cover and book design by Katie Beasley for Page Street Publishing Co.
Photography by Josh Hunt

Printed and bound in the United States

DEDICATION

This book is dedicated to my amazing family! Melanie, Makenna and Garrett, you guys have sat through countless food photography sessions waiting to eat. You have been my biggest fans and best critics.

This book would not have been possible without all your help prepping, cleaning, taste testing and giving me space to create.

I love you all so much!

CONTENTS

Foreword

Like a lot of my friends today, Josh and I originally met through social media. After all these years, I am still the man behind @meatchurch on social media, so my days are often filled with scrolling various social platforms while looking for outdoor cooking inspiration and trends. I remember vividly noticing delicious-looking food cooked on a griddle by a particular guy that was continually served up to me on Instagram. I clicked on the account and saw pages of food cooked on a griddle by this person who, fortunately for me, also happened to live in the DFW Metroplex. That guy was Josh Hunt. I immediately followed his account and shortly thereafter met Josh at one of my Meat Church events.

Josh and I hit it off immediately as he has such an infectious personality and is such a great human. We got to know each other and quickly became friends. I was so impressed with Josh and his knack for creating delicious and straight-forward recipes. He is very creative in what he creates and cooks and goes about it in a way I admire. He does his thing on the griddle and inspires others to get outside and follow suit. We have cooked together several times, and his approach is something anyone can follow and replicate.

Ultimately, I invited Josh to join my exclusive Meat Church Ambassador team to help represent my brand. This is the highest compliment I can pay anyone as the only criteria to join our team is to be noticed by myself. Josh is also the man I choose to man the griddle at each of my BBQ Schools. Having Josh at the griddle helm guarantees my recipes will be replicated just as I created them while freeing me up to spend time with my students.

As a bonus, not only can Josh make amazing creations on the griddle, but he is also a pro at grilling and smoking. He is such an accomplished outdoor cook that I know you will enjoy re-creating each recipe in this cookbook. I know I am looking forward to the fun my family will have cooking each one of these recipes together!

—**Matt Pittman**
Meat Church, Founder & CEO

Introduction

You made it! We are so glad to have you here as part of the #GriddleNation! If you are reading this book, you have more than likely already purchased your Blackstone Griddle or plan to do so in the near future. You may already be a Griddle Master looking for more recipe ideas to wow your family and friends, or you may be brand new to the wonderful art of Blackstone Griddle cooking and need some help getting started. My hope and prayer with this cookbook is that we can cover a wide gambit of Blackstone recipes to turn your griddle game into the talk of the town.

I'm so excited to share my favorite Blackstone recipes and techniques with you all. Blackstone Griddles aren't just for pancakes and burgers, although they do a dang good job at them. I have put many griddles, tools and pieces of equipment to use and will recommend some of the must-haves along the way.

Before we get to all of that, I feel it's important to talk about how I got to this point. Never in my wildest imagination would I have ever thought I would be authoring and photographing my own cookbook.

In March of 2020, the pandemic hit our world, and everything seemed to get turned on its head. Prior to this point, our family enjoyed eating out . . . maybe a little too much. When the pandemic hit and the world shut down, there was no other option than to cook at home. I have always had a passion for cooking but let the business of work and raising a family become an excuse as to why I didn't cook at home.

I work as a police detective, and we were unable to work from home like so much of the world was doing at that time. One day, while talking about what we were going to make for dinner that evening, a fellow detective recommended this new Blackstone Griddle he had recently purchased. He talked about how he could get an entire meal cooked up all at once and feed his family of four in no time. I was intrigued.

I immediately started researching Blackstone Griddles on the internet and quickly came across a model with a large 36-inch (91-cm) cooktop and two built-in air fryers. I was sold! I quickly called my wife and got the green light, with one stipulation. She said, "If you are going to spend that much, just make sure you are going use it!" I assured her I would and hit the BUY NOW button.

I picked up my new Blackstone from my local Walmart and got it put together that night. That weekend I got it seasoned up and then just stared at it. What did I cook first? Well . . . it was hamburgers and then pancakes the next morning. We've all been there . . .

Proud of my first burger off the Blackstone, I posted the picture to my Facebook account. Another friend who had been cooking on a Blackstone for a year or so recommended some Facebook groups where people get together and share their Blackstone creations and recipes. I joined the Blackstone Griddle—Recipes & Videos group run by my buddy, Andy Wilson. I was blown away by all the awesome creations being made on these griddles. Pictures of griddles full of proteins, vegetables and all the fixings filled my screen. I was hooked.

The Facebook group led me to posts from Blackstone's very own Griddle Crew. The Crew, made up of Desirée "Blackstone Betty" Ruberti-Dukes, Chef Nathan Lippy, CJ Frazier and Todd Toven, were pumping out recipes and content surrounding the Blackstone. I must have watched hours and hours of videos in that first month, trying to learn the ins and outs of cooking on a griddle. They have been a huge inspiration along this journey.

Wanting to make good on my promise to my wife to use this purchase, I decided I would cook every meal on this griddle for a month. A month turned into two, which turned into six. I was amazed at the creativity and recipes that this outdoor cooking appliance had sparked in me. Wanting to share my creations with the online community that inspired me initially, I started to study food photography and what elements make a picture of food desirable to the eye.

The same friend at work who had recommended the Blackstone to begin with recommended that I start an Instagram account to share some of my Blackstone creations. In July of 2020, what is now known as @joshhunt_griddlin was born. I found a great community of home cooks, chefs and foodies who all had a love for making and eating great food. I was captivated by just how versatile this piece of rolled cold steel became with various cooking styles and techniques. I can't wait to share the techniques I have honed, alongside sixty of some of my favorite recipes. I hope these meals become part of your regular rotation the way they have in mine as you level up your griddle game!

@joshhunt_griddlin

Josh Hunt

GRIDDLING 101

WHICH BLACKSTONE IS RIGHT FOR ME?

There are dozens of different Blackstone models on the market today, with more coming all the time. They vary by size, shape, functions and features. In this section, I'll walk you through all of the things to keep in mind as you go about selecting (or upgrading!) your Blackstone.

Size

If you are in the market for a new Blackstone, size is going to be the first factor to consider. Griddles run from 17 inches (43 cm) to 36 inches (91 cm) and every size in between. I have found that cooking for a family of four at home requires a little extra space. I have family members who don't eat meat and others who can be picky at times. The 4-heat zone, 36-inch (91-cm) model gives me plenty of room to have multiple things going at the same time, with room to spare. I also have a 22-inch (56-cm) Adventure Ready Blackstone that folds up, and it is great for taking on road trips, camping or out to the lake for a cookout. The smaller size is great for one to two people, but also works for more. My little 22-inch (56-cm) even cooked up about twenty double meat smash burgers during a football tailgate party. That being said, you should take into consideration that you may have to prepare meals in various stages, bringing it all in together at the end.

Your outdoor space is also a consideration when thinking about size. I recommend finding the dimensions of the Blackstone model you are thinking about and making sure it will fit your space before purchasing.

Features

When Blackstone first started rolling out griddles, they were just that . . . griddles. Over time, they have started to add features and functions that take outdoor cooking to a whole other level. Some models now include air fryers, range top cooktops, extra storage and even electric models that can be used inside or out. The Culinary Series of Blackstones are stylish and usually include some amazing storage options. A lot of the newer models have some type of hood. These hoods come in handy to protect the griddle from the elements and to trap heat inside for various cooking styles.

Griddle envy is real, so take some time to research the different models and pick the one that works for you.

GETTING READY TO COOK!

Before you get to griddling, I recommend purchasing an extra container of propane. It's great to have on hand if you happen to run out mid cook . . . not like it's ever happened to me . . . ok, it happens to all of us.

Let's Talk Seasoning

Properly seasoning your griddle is a crucial first step before cooking.

The griddle top is made of cold, rolled steel and needs to be protected from the elements and the moisture in your food.

It's best to clean your griddle top with warm water, light dish soap and a sponge before seasoning. Flush well with water after cleaning. This removes any leftover metal shavings and oils that may have been transferred to the griddle during manufacturing.

There are all kinds of people who will tell you how to season, but I tend to listen to the experts from Blackstone.

After washing the griddle, there will be some residual moisture. Crank all the burners on your griddle up to high, and you'll start to see the moisture wicking away as it heats up. When the griddle starts to smoke and change colors, apply an extremely light layer of oil (canola or flax seed works best for me) all over the griddle. Blackstone has developed a seasoning blend that also works great for this. I like to use a pressurized spray bottle of canola oil that helps with applying light coats. Use a pair of tongs and an old, clean dish towel to spread the oil around to all surfaces of the griddle. Be careful, the griddle and oil are extremely hot. Don't forget the sides and back walls, front and back. Any exposed griddle surface needs oil.

> **NOTE**
>
> Make sure not to leave anything that could melt in the side shelves, close to the griddle. Heat rises from the griddle and will melt anything you put there—don't ask me how I know.

As the oil starts to smoke, you'll see the griddle go from a gray color, to brown and eventually to black. After 10 to 15 minutes, the oil will stop smoking. Time to add another extremely light layer of oil across the griddle surfaces. Once again, when the griddle stops smoking, add another layer. Repeat for a total of five to six rounds of seasoning. As you do, you are building up a nonstick layer of protection for your griddle.

After five or six rounds of seasoning, turn your griddle off and allow it to cool. Your griddle will continue to season the more you cook on it. I recommended a spray bottle of canola oil for adding a light layer of oil to the griddle before and after each cook.

I also recommend watching some Blackstone seasoning videos on YouTube before you start.

The Prep

I can't stress how important prepping your ingredients ahead of time is. You'll learn that everything cooks up pretty fast on a Blackstone. Having everything ready before you start can keep you from taking the "walk of shame" and running back into the house for forgotten ingredients. We all do it! I'm usually hollering for the kids to bring something I forgot, so I don't have to take my eyes off the griddle. You'll have a much better experience if you prep ahead, trust me.

Low and Slow

I always recommend to my friends to start out your griddle journey with your temperatures low and slow. As you advance your skills and learn your griddle's quirky hot spots, you'll gradually start to increase your temps and lower your cooking times. Take it from someone who burned a lot of dishes early on!

TAKING CARE OF YOUR GRIDDLE

As I talked about earlier, models with hoods are great for protecting your griddle from the elements. A good waterproof grill cover is another option if your griddle will be out in the rain, snow or in a humid climate. If possible, get your griddle under a covered area and make sure to shut the propane off when not in use.

Cleaning the griddle after a cook is really easy. A good scraper is key—any of the Blackstone brand scrapers work great. After cooking, and while the griddle is still warm, lightly scrape all remaining food debris from the griddle top and into the rear grease trap. Make sure not to put too much pressure on the scraper as it can gouge or peel up the seasoning. I like to use blue, shop-style paper towels to wipe up any remaining oils or bits of food, pushing it all to the rear grease trap. While it's still warm, I will then add a light layer of oil, and my griddle is ready for the next cook.

If you happen to cook something sticky, you can turn your griddle heat up to medium-high heat and squirt some water onto the griddle. The water will steam and allow the sticky substances to come off the griddle much easier. However, too much water, or water used after every cooking session, can cause the seasoning to weaken and break apart.

The rest of the griddle can be cleaned with just about anything. I like to use a damp dish towel and an all-natural citrus-based grill cleaner to keep the side shelves and exterior nice and clean. You'll also want to keep an eye on your rear grease trap. I recommend using the Blackstone aluminum liners for easier cleaning and disposal.

ESSENTIAL EQUIPMENT

There are hundreds of Blackstone accessories out there. From spatulas to pizza ovens, you name it, they've got it! Getting started, there's a few pieces of equipment that I highly recommend along with the scraper mentioned earlier.

Spatulas

Spatulas are more than likely going to be your most-used tool. I recommend at least two. They are going to be your flipping, chopping, stirring and smashing friends for the rest of this griddle journey. I personally like spatulas that have plastic and silicone handles that allow me to throw them in the dishwasher.

Tongs

A good set of tongs is crucial for moving food around on the griddle or plating dishes. Dads, make sure to always click the tongs at least twice before every use.

Burger Smasher

We have several smash burger recipes coming up. A good burger smasher is a great tool to keep on hand. There are lots of different styles with various sizes and handles. Two of my favorites come from @theburgersmasher, and I also have a custom smasher from @muleskinnersmokerigs. Smashers can also be used as panini presses or steak weights, among many other things.

Warming Rack

Something as simple as a warming rack and a dome or hood can take your cooking experience on the Blackstone to whole new levels. Elevating your ingredients off direct heat allows you to thoroughly cook dishes without burning the ingredients. A dome or hood allows you to trap heat inside, with oven-like results. We'll use them several times through this book, so I highly recommend having them on hand.

Instant-Read Meat Thermometer

Throughout my culinary journey one tool has improved my food more than anything. A good instant-read meat thermometer is amazing and takes the guess-work out of preparing proteins. Blackstone makes a model that has an instant-read temperature probe on one side and an infrared surface thermometer on the other for accurate temperature readings of your griddle top. It works great and is super affordable!

GRIDDLE COOKING STYLES

When most people hear "griddle," they think Waffle House and the kind of food you'd expect from Waffle House, but the truth is, griddles are used in almost every restaurant on the planet. From the greasiest dives to the swankiest steak houses, griddles are amazing culinary tools.

Throughout my time cooking on the Blackstone griddle, I've found methods like searing, sautéing, shallow frying, deep-frying and even indirect cooking are possible.

The griddle is a big heat-conducting surface. Heat-safe pots, pans and skillets work great. Cast iron may be my favorite to use on the griddle top.

We'll use most of these cooking techniques as we traverse the various recipes in this book!

BLACKSTONE SUPPORT CREW

Since starting my Instagram and Facebook pages, I often feel like I should be wearing a headset and sitting behind a computer at Blackstone Customer Support. I get tons of questions about all things Blackstone, and I'm happy to answer them. If you ever have any questions about anything related to griddle cooking, the recipes in this book or just want to say hi, please don't be shy. Hit me up on Instagram @joshhunt_griddlin or on Facebook @joshhuntgriddlin—I'd love to chat.

Now let's get to griddling!

OVER-THE-TOP BLACKSTONE BURGERS

I couldn't write a Blackstone cookbook and not start it off with a chapter on burgers! Let's face it, Blackstone does it better than anyone—from smash burgers to big and beefy, nothing beats a burger searing on a griddle and cooking in its own juices. This chapter includes some of my favorite recipes in the book, like the Oklahoma Smash Burgers (page 21) and the Southwestern Green Chile Smash Burgers (page 22). As you can see from the variety of recipes in this chapter, you can take these burgers in so many different flavor directions. But enough talking, let's get to smashing!

Oklahoma Smash Burgers

When I think of a smash burger, this is what comes to mind! What makes them Oklahoma Smash Burgers you ask? The act of smashing the onions into the meat during the cooking process is what sets these apart from other smashers. The simplicity of the ingredients makes these amazingly easy to cook. People like Mike Puma at the @GothamBurgerSocialClub and George Motz have made these burgers a staple across the country. Now, you'll have all the secrets to make these burgers in your very own backyard!

MAKES 4 BURGERS

Let's start by cranking your lightly oiled Blackstone griddle top to high heat.

Thinly slice the onion. You are going to want these as paper-thin as you can get them. A mandolin slicer works great for this.

Loosely roll the ground chuck into 2-ounce (56-g) meatballs. Place the meatballs on the blazing hot griddle. Place approximately a quarter of the thinly sliced onion over the top of each meatball. It's okay if some fall off to the side.

Use your burger smasher to press the meatballs and onion flat. You may want to use a piece of parchment paper between the smasher and meatball to keep it from sticking. As you smash each meatball, hold down for approximately 10 seconds. This pressure helps make sure you are getting a good sear.

Season the patty with a pinch of salt and black pepper (approximately a ¼ teaspoon of both). Allow the patties to cook for 2 to 3 minutes. You will see juices start to rise up through the patty and the edges start to brown. That's your indication that it's time to flip. It might feel stuck, but that's the crispy layer of the smash burger.

Once flipped, cut the heat on the griddle all the way to low and let the residual heat carry over. Add a slice of American cheese to each patty. Stack the patties two high and add a swirl of ketchup and yellow mustard plus 4 slices of dill pickle to the top of each.

Add the top of the bun, with the bottom bun on top of that (as seen in the picture). This will allow the buns to steam a bit and warm as the burger finishes cooking.

Once the cheese is melted, a minute or two later, the burger is done. Remove the bottom bun and stack the rest of the burger on top.

Serve with your favorite fries or chips.

1 large white onion

1 lb (454 g) 80/20 ground chuck (2 [2-oz (56-g)] patties per burger)

Pinch of salt and ground black pepper

8 slices of American cheese

Ketchup

Yellow mustard

16 dill pickle slices

4 potato roll hamburger buns

Fries or chips, for serving

Southwestern Green Chile Smash Burgers

Green chiles make everything better in my opinion! I must fight the urge to make this exact burger on a weekly basis. It's that good! Don't let the green chiles scare you. They pack a subtle kick of spice but are super flavorful.

MAKES 4 BURGERS

Start by cranking your lightly oiled Blackstone griddle top to high heat. While the griddle heats up, smear a teaspoon of mayonnaise on each bun and place them face down on the griddle. Toast for 3 to 5 minutes, or until lightly browned, and then remove them from the griddle.

Loosely roll the ground chuck into 2-ounce (56-g) meatballs. Place the meatballs on the blazing hot griddle.

Use your burger press to smash the meatballs flat. You may want to use a piece of parchment paper between the smasher and meatball to keep it from sticking. As you smash each meatball, hold down for approximately 10 seconds. This pressure helps makes sure you are getting a good sear.

Season each patty with a pinch of salt and black pepper (approximately a ¼ teaspoon of both). For an added kick of flavor, you can substitute your favorite spicy seasoning here.

Allow the patties to cook for 2 to 3 minutes. You will start to see juices rising up through the patty and the edges starting to brown. That's your indication that it's time to flip. It might feel stuck, but that's the crispy layer of the smash burger.

Once flipped, cut the heat on the griddle all the way to low and let the residual heat carry over. Add a slice of pepper Jack cheese to each patty. After about 2 more minutes, stack the patties two high.

While the burgers are finishing, add the green chiles to the griddle top, letting the residual heat warm them. When they start to bubble, add 1 ounce (28 g) of green chiles to each burger.

Once the cheese is melted, a minute or two later, the burger is done. Stack the burger patties on your toasted brioche bun and top with your favorite condiments; mine is mayonnaise.

Serve with your favorite fries or chips.

4 tsp (20 ml) mayonnaise, plus more for topping

4 brioche hamburger buns

1 lb (454 g) 80/20 ground chuck (2 [2-oz (56-g)] patties per burger)

Pinch of salt and ground black pepper (sub your favorite spicy seasoning)

8 slices of pepper Jack cheese

4 oz (113 g) diced flame-roasted green chiles

Fries or chips, for serving

Asian Fusion Smash Burgers

I love fusion food! Ingredients or styles that aren't normally thought of together getting mashed into a delicious, unexpected recipe—you just can't beat it. The umami flavor of the mushrooms combined with the sweet barbeque sauce gives you all the essence you'd expect from your favorite Japanese dish fused with all of the textures you've come to expect from a gourmet burger. I'm pretty partial to this burger as I won an online food contest with the idea and photography through Food Beast. Winning that competition opened up lots of relationships and opportunities with fellow content creators and chefs. I'll forever be grateful for this amazing smash burger! Now it's your turn to see where it can take you.

MAKES 2 BURGERS

Let's set your lightly oiled griddle to medium-high heat. Spread ½ tablespoon (7 ml) of Japanese mayonnaise on the insides of each hamburger bun. Place the mayo side of the buns down on the medium-high heat until toasted golden brown, 3 to 4 minutes. Remove the buns from the heat.

While the buns are toasting, sauté the mushrooms in the butter. Season the mushrooms with a pinch of black pepper and 2 tablespoons (30 ml) of Bachan's Japanese BBQ Sauce. Continue to toss the mushrooms for 3 to 4 minutes, or until soft and slightly browned. Once done, slide the mushrooms to the side of the griddle or remove.

Ball up the ground chuck into about 2-ounce (56-g) balls. Add the meatballs to the medium-high heat griddle. Use your burger press to smash the meatballs flat. You may want to use a piece of parchment paper between the smasher and meatball to keep it from sticking. As you smash each meatball, hold down for approximately 10 seconds. This pressure helps makes sure you are getting a good sear.

I season each burger patty with a pinch of salt and black pepper along with about ½ tablespoon (7 ml) of the Bachan's BBQ sauce. Allow to cook; you will start to see juice rising up through the patty and the edges starting to brown. After 2 to 3 minutes, scrape up the patty and flip over. It might feel stuck, but that's the crispy layer of the smash burger.

Once flipped, cut the heat on the griddle all the way to low and let the residual heat carry over. Add a slice of white Cheddar cheese to each patty. After about 2 more minutes, stack the patties two high. Add the double stacked beef patties to the buns. Add a shake of that Japanese furikake, a pinch of chopped green onions and the sautéed mushrooms to each burger. Add some additional Japanese mayonnaise to the burger crown and add it to the top of your burger.

Take a couple of pictures for "The Gram" (that's Instagram, Mom) and enjoy with your favorite fries, chips or tater tots!

4 tbsp (60 ml) Japanese mayonnaise, divided

2 hamburger buns

5 oz (141 g) shiitake mushrooms, cleaned and sliced

3 tbsp (42 g) unsalted butter

Pinch of salt and ground black pepper, divided

4 tbsp (60 ml) Bachan's Japanese BBQ Sauce (sub your favorite teriyaki sauce), divided

½ lb (226 g) 80/20 ground chuck (2 [2-oz (56-g)]) patties per burger)

4 slices of white Cheddar cheese

2 tsp (3 g) Japanese furikake seasoning (seaweed and sesame seed mix)

1 bunch green onions, chopped

Fries, chips or tater tots, for serving

Jalapeño & Onion Triple Smash Burgers

Smash burgers have become a staple around our house. From the simplest of ingredients, a masterpiece can be created that comes together super quick and will wow the toughest food critic. You can take these burgers in all sorts of different directions by tweaking the ingredients. This is one of my absolute favorite variations, thanks to the spicy kick of jalapeño cooled off with the tangy, homemade sauce. That, combined with the gooey cheese and bold beef flavor, makes for one incredible bite.

MAKES 4 BURGERS

First, make the Big Smack Sauce. In a bowl, mix the mayonnaise, ketchup, sweet relish, yellow mustard, onion powder and vinegar together well and refrigerate until ready to use.

Start off by slowly sautéing the onion and jalapeños on a lightly oiled medium-heat griddle zone. Season the veggies with a teaspoon of Meat Church Holy Cow seasoning. Make sure to toss the veggies around every minute or so. Cut the heat off once the onion starts to become translucent, 4 to 5 minutes.

While the veggies sauté, toast the inside of your buns on the same burners set to medium. This should only take about 2 minutes. If you are cooking on a 36-inch (91-cm) griddle, you'll want to set the other half of your griddle to high in preparation for the burger patties. If you are on a smaller sized Blackstone, you may have to complete these steps in batches.

(continued)

BIG SMACK SAUCE

1 cup (240 ml) Duke's Mayonnaise

¼ cup (60 ml) ketchup

¼ cup (60 g) sweet relish

1 tbsp (15 ml) yellow mustard

2 tsp (5 g) onion powder

1 tsp vinegar

Jalapeño & Onion Triple Smash Burgers (continued)

For the patties, roll the ground chuck loosely into twelve, 2-ounce (56-g) balls, about the size of a racquetball. Place the meatballs on the blazing hot griddle. I like to let one side of the meatball brown for about 30 seconds, then I flip them before smashing them down. The seared side keeps the smasher from sticking to the meat.

Using a flat spatula or a burger smasher, smash the meatballs down as flat as you can get them and hold for 10 to 12 seconds. Repeat for each meatball. Season each smashed patty with about a ¼ teaspoon of the Meat Church Holy Cow seasoning.

Allow the patties to cook for 2 to 3 minutes. You will start to see juices rising up through the patty and the edges starting to brown. That's your indication that it's time to flip. It might feel stuck, but that's the crispy layer of the smash burger.

Once flipped, cut your griddle heat down to low and let the residual heat carry over. Add a slice of Colby Jack cheese to each patty. Once the cheese is melted (a minute or two later), the smashed patties will be done cooking.

Build your burger on the bottom bun, with the desired number of patties. As the name implies, I typically use three for mine! Top the smashed patties with the sautéed onion, jalapeño and a spoonful of the Big Smack burger sauce. Crown the burgers with the top buns and serve.

SMASH BURGERS

1 medium white onion, thinly sliced

2 large jalapeños, sliced (seeds removed for less heat)

5 tsp (12 g) Meat Church Holy Cow seasoning (sub your favorite burger seasoning mix), divided

4 hamburger buns

2 lb (907 g) 80/20 ground chuck (3 [2-oz (56-g)]) patties per burger)

12 slices Colby Jack cheese

Texas Smashed Patty Melts

Two of my favorite burger styles, the smash burger and the patty melt, come together here in one gloriously delicious burger! The Texas toast is really what sets this burger apart. It's toasty and crunchy on the outside and soft and pillowy on the inside. Get ready to wow the family with some amazing burgers off the Blackstone!

MAKES 4 PATTY MELTS

Let's start off with your lightly oiled Blackstone set to low heat. Add the bacon slices to the griddle and let them cook low and slow, flipping every minute or so. I have found this is the best way to get perfect bacon without burning it. After 8 to 10 minutes of flipping, remove the bacon once it's just about your desired crispiness. It will continue to crisp up once removed from the heat.

Once the bacon is cooked, set the griddle to medium heat.

Spread about a teaspoon of mayonnaise on one side of each slice of Texas toast. Lay the toast mayo side down on the griddle until lightly toasted, 2 to 3 minutes. Make sure to check on it every 30 seconds or so, so it doesn't burn. Once one side is toasted, remove them from the griddle.

Turn your griddle up to high. Loosely roll the ground chuck into 2-ounce (56-g) meatballs, about the size of a racquetball. Place the meatballs on the blazing hot griddle.

Use your burger press to smash the meatballs flat. You may want to use a piece of parchment paper between the smasher and meatball to keep it from sticking. As you smash each meatball, hold down for approximately 10 seconds. This pressure helps makes sure you are getting a good sear.

Season each patty with about a teaspoon of Blackstone's Whiskey Burger seasoning, shaken over the top.

8 slices of bacon

8 tsp (40 ml) mayonnaise, plus more for topping

8 slices of thick Texas toast (thick cut white bread)

1 lb (454 g) 80/20 ground chuck (2 [2-oz (56-g)] patties per patty melt)

8 tsp (12 g) Blackstone's Whiskey Burger or Pub Burger Seasoning (sub your favorite burger seasoning)

(continued)

Texas Smashed Patty Melts (continued)

As the patties are cooking, add the diced white onion to the side of the griddle. The residual heat should get these sautéed up nice. Make sure to stir every 30 seconds or so. Once ready, push them off to a corner of the griddle to stay warm.

As the burger patties cook, you will start to see the juice rising up through the patty and the edges starting to brown. After 2 to 3 minutes, scrape up the patty and flip over. It might feel stuck, but that's the crispy layer of the smash burger.

Once flipped, cut the heat on the griddle all the way to low and let the residual heat carry over. Add a slice of white American cheese to each patty. After about 2 more minutes, stack the patties two high.

Place the double stack of patties on the untoasted side of one slice of Texas toast. Add a good amount of sautéed onions, two slices of bacon and whatever condiment you like best (I went with mayonnaise). Top with the last slice of Texas toast and serve up with some fries, tots or chips.

1 medium white onion, diced

8 slices of white American cheese

Fries, tater tots or chips, for serving

Hunka Hunka Burnin' Love Burgers

Sometimes you must push the boundaries! That's exactly what we did with this big, delicious, spicy burger. It's got layer after layer of spicy goodness on top of some high-quality chuck brisket and short rib beef patties, making for an amazing burger.

MAKES 2 BURGERS

Let's start by making a chipotle aioli to top these burgers. Take two of the chipotle peppers in adobo sauce and give them a mince. In a bowl, stir in the chipotles with the mayonnaise and combine well. (Reserve the rest of the chipotles for another recipe.)

Set the lightly oiled griddle to medium-high heat. Add the butter, spreading it out with a spatula. Toast the brioche buns in the butter for 2 to 3 minutes, until golden brown. Once toasted, remove them from the heat.

Season your beef patties with the Meat Church Holy Voodoo seasoning and a pinch of black pepper. Add the patties to a lightly oiled medium-high griddle. Allow to cook for 3 to 4 minutes per side, until it reaches your desired doneness.

As the beef patties cook, add the two whole jalapeños and sliced jalapeño to the griddle, flipping every minute until all sides are seared. Add two slices of pepper Jack cheese to each beef patty. Pour a tablespoon (15 ml) of water on the griddle and close your hood to allow the cheese to melt.

Build your burger with a lettuce leaf underneath two burger patties. The lettuce will help prevent the bun from getting soggy. Top your burgers with the crispy fried onions, jalapeño slices and a spoon of the chipotle aioli. Use a bamboo stake to top your burger bun off with a seared jalapeño so everyone knows what kind of burger they are in for.

Serve with your favorite fries or tots.

CHIPOTLE AIOLI

¼ cup (60 ml) mayonnaise

1 (7.5-oz [212-g]) can chipotle peppers in adobo sauce

BURGERS

2 tbsp (28 g) unsalted butter

2 brioche split top buns

4 (¼-lb [113-g]) chuck brisket and short rib beef patties (store-bought, sub any ¼-lb [113-g] beef patties)

4 tsp (10 g) Meat Church Holy Voodoo seasoning (sub your favorite spicy seasoning)

Pinch of ground black pepper

3 large jalapeños (two whole, one sliced)

8 slices pepper Jack cheese

2 large lettuce leaves

¼ cup (26 g) crispy fried onions

Fries or tater tots, for serving

BBQ & Bacon Blackstone Burgers

We love smash burgers, but sometimes you just need a thick burger piled high! These burgers will help with any BBQ cravings you may have. The sweet BBQ sauce and crispy onion rings will make your burgers legendary at the next block party.

MAKES 2 BURGERS

Start by turning your lightly oiled Blackstone griddle up to medium-high heat.

As your griddle warms up, place the 4 frozen onion rings into the Blackstone air fryer set to medium. After approximately 8 minutes, the onion rings should be nice and crispy. Remove them from the heat. If you don't have a Blackstone model with the air fryer, you can always prepare the onion rings in a separate air fryer, toaster oven or conventional oven in the same fashion.

Rub the inside of your hamburger buns with ½ teaspoon of mayonnaise on each side.

Once the griddle heat is up, place the buns face down on the griddle. Toast the buns for 2 to 3 minutes, or until they are golden brown. Remove and set aside.

Season your brisket burger patties with a teaspoon of the Meat Church Holy Cow seasoning on each side. Place the patties on the hot griddle. Allow the burgers to brown and sear, flipping every 2 minutes or so, until your desired doneness is reached. It should take 8 to 10 minutes for a medium-well finish.

As the burgers are cooking, place your diced white onion near the cooking burgers on the griddle top. The rendered fat coming from the burgers works great to help caramelize the onions. Frequently stir the onions until they become translucent.

When the burgers are close to being done, cut your griddle heat down to low and let the residual heat carry over. Top each burger with a slice of the Cheddar cheese. Close your hood or place a dome on the burgers to help the cheese melt.

As the cheese melts, start to build your burgers. Place the lettuce leaf on the bottom bun and top with a slice of tomato. The lettuce will help keep the bottom bun from getting soggy. Place a cheesy burger patty on the top of the tomato and lettuce. Add two crispy onion rings and top with a tablespoon (15 ml) of BBQ sauce. Add half of your sautéed diced onion to the top and crown it off with that top bun.

We like these served up with some crispy BBQ-flavored kettle-cooked potato chips.

4 frozen onion rings

2 brioche sesame seed hamburger buns

2 tsp (10 ml) mayonnaise

2 (5-oz [141-g]) brisket/chuck burger patties

4 tsp (10 g) Meat Church Holy Cow seasoning (sub your favorite BBQ rub)

1 small white onion, diced

2 slices Cheddar cheese

2 lettuce leaves

1 tomato, sliced

2 tbsp (30 ml) BBQ sauce

BBQ-flavored kettle-cooked chips, for serving

TASTY TEX-MEX TACOS & MORE

I have lived and traveled all over the great state of Texas and have been influenced by the food and culture from El Paso to Texarkana. The dishes in this chapter are inspired by those foods and cultures that have helped shape me into the cook I am today. Spicy, savory and sweet tend to meld together in these dishes and explode with flavor! This chapter includes some quick and easy meals, like the Crispy Beef & Green Chile Tacos (page 38) and Voodoo Shrimp Quesadillas (page 48), as well as meals that take some time and patience to get the textures and flavors just right, like the Beef Birria Tacos (page 42) and Griddled Sweet Corn Tamale Cakes (page 45)—but the extra effort is well worth the show-stopping taste! I think you're going like what we have in store.

Crispy Beef & Green Chile Tacos

No meal takes me back to my childhood like crispy tacos. A weekly staple in our home, these crunchy and spicy tacos can be taken in so many different directions with various toppings and fillings. The simplicity of these power-packed ingredients makes this a perfect weekday meal to throw together after a busy day.

MAKES 12 TACOS

Turn your lightly oiled griddle to medium-high heat. When the griddle gets up to temp, add the ground beef and break it apart with a spatula. About 5 minutes into the cook, add the taco seasoning to the beef and combine well. Continuously toss the ground beef for 8 to 10 minutes, or until browned.

Once browned, add the green chiles to the beef and combine. Turn the heat off and leave the beef on the griddle top to stay warm.

Separate the beef mixture into crispy taco shells. Top the tacos with shredded cheese, shredded lettuce, diced tomatoes and a drizzle of creamy chipotle sauce.

We serve these tacos up with yellow Spanish rice and refried beans.

1 lb (454 g) 90/10 ground beef

4 tbsp (20 g) taco seasoning

3 oz (85 g) flame-roasted diced green chiles

12 crispy corn taco shells

2 oz (56 g) shredded Mexican cheese

Shredded lettuce

1 (10-oz [283-g]) can diced tomatoes, drained

1½ cups (360 ml) creamy chipotle sauce

Spanish rice and refried beans, for serving

Tequila Lime Shrimp & Salmon Tacos

The Adventure Ready 22-inch (56-cm) Blackstone goes just about anywhere we go on road trips. We've found that bringing along some tortillas, proteins and veggies means we can have a quick and easy meal in all kinds of beautiful locations. These tacos were griddled up on the back porch of a lake house overlooking beautiful Lake Hamilton in Arkansas but could be made just as well on your model of Blackstone, wherever you are.

MAKES 6 TACOS

First, let's dry the salmon with a paper towel. If we leave a bunch of excess moisture on the fillet, we will not get a great sear. Add a coat of olive oil to all sides of each salmon piece and season with a teaspoon or so of Blackstone's Tequila Lime seasoning on all sides.

Repeat the same process with the shrimp. Pat dry, lightly oil and season them up with the remainder of the Blackstone Tequila Lime seasoning.

Turn your griddle to medium-high heat and apply a light layer of cooking spray across the surface. After approximately 5 minutes, add your raw flour tortillas to the griddle top. As they cook, you'll start to see them change color and start to bubble up a bit. After 2 minutes, give them a flip. Now the tortillas will start to really balloon up as the steam gets trapped inside. You can give them a bit of a gentle smash to flatten them back out. After 4 to 5 minutes total cook time, you should start to start to see small brown spots on both sides. Go ahead and remove the tortillas from the heat and keep them warm in a tortilla warmer or between two plates.

Next, add your salmon fillets to the griddle. Allow them to cook undisturbed for 3 to 4 minutes and then flip. You should start to see a nice sear and an almost blackened finish. Allow the other side to cook for 3 to 4 minutes and then break the salmon into bite-sized pieces. This is a great time to check the center of the salmon and see if it's done to your liking. When it's done, you can either remove it from the griddle or slide it over to a burner that's off or set to low.

Give your griddle a scrape, utilizing that rear grease trap, and give it a fresh, light coat of cooking spray. Add the shrimp to the medium-high griddle top and allow them to cook for approximately 90 seconds before flipping. Let them go another 90 seconds, or until they are pink and no longer translucent. The shrimp will also start to curl in on themselves once they are done. Cut your heat. Combine the salmon and shrimp on the griddle.

It's time to build your tacos! On each tortilla add a ½ ounce (14 g) of the shredded coleslaw, shrimp and salmon, and top with your favorite salsa or crema sauce. Garnish with a squeeze of lime and a sprinkle of chopped cilantro.

3 (5-oz [141-g]) skinless pink Atlantic salmon fillets

4 tbsp (60 ml) olive oil

3 tbsp (15 g) Blackstone Tequila Lime seasoning (sub your favorite southwest seasoning), divided

½ lb (226 g) raw peeled/deveined shrimp

6 fajita-sized, raw flour tortillas

1 (8-oz [226-g]) package shredded tricolored coleslaw

Salsa, or your favorite crema sauce

Quartered limes and chopped cilantro, for garnish

Beef Birria Tacos

This is one of those recipes that can take all afternoon and utilizes some extra equipment, but the result is well worth the time and effort you put into it. The spicy beef combined with the melty cheese is what dreams are made of! When you tie that in with a crispy tortilla and a flavor-packing broth to dip it all in, you'll wonder why it ever took you so long to make these! Birria is traditionally made with goat meat and comes from the Jalisco region of Mexico.

MAKES 12–24 TACOS

Let's start by setting your lightly oiled griddle to high heat. If you're on a 28-inch (71-cm) model or smaller you may want to turn all the burners to high. If you're on a 36-inch (91-cm) model, the two middle burners set to high should do the trick.

Go ahead and season all sides of the sirloin beef tip roast quarters with Meat Church Holy Voodoo seasoning and let it rest on the counter as your griddle comes up to temperature.

When your Blackstone is blazing hot, sear each side of the roast pieces for about 60 seconds each. This searing, also known as the Maillard reaction, is causing the outer layer of the meat to caramelize as the sugars and amino acids react with each other. It will result in an a more distinctive beef flavor profile in the end product.

Once all sides are seared, remove the roast pieces from the heat and allow them to rest.

(continued)

BEEF

4 lb (1.8 kg) beef sirloin tip roast, cut into quarters

2 tbsp (14 g) Meat Church Holy Voodoo seasoning (sub your favorite spicy beef seasoning)

Beef Birria Tacos (continued)

Let's get to work on that birria broth, also known as consommé. In a medium-sized pot, bring the beef broth to a boil on a burner set to high (this can be accomplished on your Blackstone or on a separate stove, depending on the size of your Blackstone). As it's coming to a boil, add all the dried chilies with the seeds and stems removed. Also add the can of chipotles in adobo sauce, garlic, oregano, cumin, coriander, cayenne, Meat Church Holy Voodoo seasoning, cinnamon stick and bay leaf. Stir until well combined. Once the broth comes to a boil, reduce the heat to low and let it simmer until the dried chilies have softened, about 30 minutes. I like to remove the cinnamon stick after 10 minutes, as it starts to fall apart after a while.

Once the broth has simmered on low for about 30 minutes, add a can of diced tomatoes and mix. Remove the bay leaf. In batches, add the broth-and-tomato mixture to a blender. Blend for 2 to 3 minutes per batch, until completely smooth. Add the blended broth into the Instant Pot or pressure cooker. Add a quarter of your chopped onions, the sliced carrots and your seared beef roast. Add water to the pot until the beef is covered.

Add the top to the pressure cooker, making sure it's sealed well. We're going to cook this on high pressure. Once the cooker pressure is up, cook for 55 minutes. At the 55-minute mark, safely release the pressure. Remove the beef and shred it with a pair of forks. It should just fall apart at that point.

It's time to make some tacos! You'll want to have the consommé close by the griddle. I will usually remove the metal pot from the Instant Pot and set it on the griddle's side shelf. Set the rest of the remaining ingredients close by as well.

Set the lightly oiled griddle to medium heat. With a pair of tongs, dip the corn tortillas in the birria broth and place them on the griddle. The size of your Blackstone will determine how many batches of tacos you can make. After a minute or so, flip the tortillas. Top each with a portion of the shredded beef, shredded Oaxaca cheese, chopped cilantro and onion from the broth to taste.

Fold the tacos over and ladle some broth over each taco. Allow them to cook another 3 to 4 minutes per side, flipping every 2 minutes or so. You'll want to remove them when the cheese is melty and the tortillas start to brown.

Repeat these steps until all the tacos are cooked. Serve these up with a side bowl of the consommé to dip with extra cilantro and the remaining onions as desired!

BIRRIA CONSOMMÉ

4 cups (960 ml) beef broth

6 dried California chiles, seeds and stems removed

6 dried adobo chiles, seeds and stems removed

3 dried chiles de arbol, seeds and stems removed

1 (7-oz [199-g]) can chipotle peppers in adobo sauce

2 cloves garlic, minced

1 tbsp (6 g) dried oregano flakes

1 tbsp (6 g) cumin

1 tbsp (5 g) coriander

1 tbsp (5 g) cayenne

1 tbsp (7 g) Meat Church Holy Voodoo seasoning

1 cinnamon stick

1 bay leaf

1 (14-oz [392-g]) can diced tomatoes, drained

2 medium white or red onions, chopped, divided

1 cup (128 g) sliced baby carrots

ASSEMBLY

24 taco-sized corn tortillas (white or yellow)

20 oz (566 g) Oaxaca cheese, shredded

2 heads cilantro, chopped

SPECIAL EQUIPMENT

Instant Pot/Pressure Cooker

Griddled Sweet Corn Tamale Cakes

With my wife being a vegetarian, I'm always looking for ways to make creative and delicious veggie options for her. These tamale cakes are a great option and taste awesome! The sweet corn in this otherwise spicy and savory dish makes it pop. They were inspired by an appetizer we had while out to eat but are hearty enough to make an entire meal.

MAKES 2 SERVINGS (3 CORN CAKES EACH)

Let's start by making the Southwestern Sauce. Mix the mayonnaise, vinegar, water, sugar, chili powder, paprika, cayenne pepper, onion powder and garlic powder together in a bowl until well combined. Place the sauce into a squeeze bottle and keep it chilled.

To make the pico de gallo, in a large bowl, mix together the onion, jalapeño, lime juice, sea salt, tomatoes and cilantro. Keep it chilled as well.

Let's get to those sweet corn tamale cakes by pulsing 1 cup (154 g) of the frozen corn in a food processor until it's coarsely pureed. Place the pureed corn into a large mixing bowl with the sugar, salt and butter. Mix until well combined.

In the same bowl, add the flour and masa. Mix until no flour is visible. Mix in the remaining 2 cups (308 g) of whole frozen corn kernels.

Use a ½-cup (120-ml) measuring cup to portion out the corn cake mixture.

(continued)

SOUTHWESTERN SAUCE

½ cup (120 ml) mayonnaise

1 tsp white vinegar

1 tsp water

1 tsp sugar

½ tsp chili powder

¼ tsp paprika

⅛ tsp cayenne pepper

¼ tsp onion powder

⅛ tsp garlic powder

PICO DE GALLO

1 cup (160 g) white onion, finely chopped

1 jalapeño, ribs and seeds removed, finely chopped

¼ cup (60 ml) lime juice

¼ tsp sea salt, plus more to taste

1½ lb (680 g) ripe red tomatoes, chopped

1 cup (16 g) fresh cilantro, freshly chopped, divided (about 2 bunches), plus extra for topping

Griddled Sweet Corn Tamale Cakes (continued)

Use your hands to form the portions into 3-inch (8-cm)-wide patties. If the patties are not wanting to stay together, add a tablespoon or two (15 to 30 ml) of water to the mix until they do. Place the patties onto a baking sheet with parchment paper.

Turn your griddle to medium-low heat and spread the olive oil out across your cooking surface. Once the griddle is up to temperature, remove the cakes from the parchment paper and add them to the griddle. Shallow-fry the patties until they are golden brown on the bottom, 5 to 8 minutes. Flip and continue to cook for another 5 to 8 minutes, until the other side is golden brown as well. Remove the cakes from the heat.

Place the tomatillo salsa in a microwave safe bowl and cook it in the microwave for 1 to 2 minutes, until warmed.

On two serving plates, lay a tamale corn husk down flat. Spoon about a ½ cup (120 ml) of the warmed tomatillo salsa on the plate and add three corn cakes to each plate. Top each corn cake with a dollop of sour cream, pico de gallo, diced avocado and chopped cilantro to taste.

Drizzle some of the southwestern sauce over each corn cake and serve hot.

CORN CAKE

3 cups (462 g) frozen sweet corn, divided

6 tbsp (90 g) sugar

¼ tsp salt

1 cup (228 g) unsalted butter, softened to room temperature

4 tbsp (32 g) all-purpose flour

1 cup (125 g) corn masa harina flour

4 tbsp (60 ml) olive oil

GARNISH

16 oz (454 g) tomatillo salsa verde, for serving

2 tamale corn husks, for serving, optional

16 oz (454 g) sour cream, for garnish, to taste

1 avocado, diced, for serving

Voodoo Shrimp Quesadillas

Quesadillas might just be the easiest, but most rewarding creation on the Blackstone. Crunchy, cheesy, spicy and savory all come together to make your tastebuds dance! They make an awesome vessel for your favorite dips and salsas.

MAKES 2 QUESADILLAS

Start by mixing the onion, jalapeño, lime juice, sea salt, tomatoes and cilantro together in a large bowl until well combined. Place in the refrigerator until ready to use.

Use a paper towel to dry the shrimp. In a bowl, place the shrimp and avocado oil and mix until the shrimp are covered. Season with the Meat Church Holy Voodoo seasoning and stir to combine.

Turn two burners up to medium-high heat on your lightly oiled Blackstone. Once up to temp, add the shrimp to the griddle. Toss them around with a spatula for 3 to 4 minutes until they start to curl and are no longer translucent. Remove the shrimp from the heat.

Scrape the griddle and add a light layer of oil. Add your tortillas and let them warm for about 60 seconds. Flip and start to build your quesadillas. To each tortilla center, add half of the shrimp, ¼ cup (45 g) of pico de gallo (drain any excess juice), half a sliced avocado and ½ cup (57 g) of shredded Oaxaca cheese.

Fold two sides of the tortilla over the center, as if you're making an open-ended burrito. Carefully flip the quesadillas over every minute or so, until the cheese is melty, and the tortillas get toasty, 3 to 4 minutes.

Remove the quesadillas from the heat and let them rest a minute. Slice each into quarters.

Serve with Spanish rice, additional pico de gallo and your favorite salsa or guacamole.

PICO DE GALLO

1 cup (160 g) finely chopped white onion

1 jalapeño, ribs and seeds removed, finely chopped

¼ cup (60 ml) lime juice

¼ tsp sea salt, plus more to taste

1½ lb (680 g) ripe red tomatoes, chopped

½ cup (8 g) freshly chopped fresh cilantro (about 1 bunch)

QUESADILLAS

1 lb (454 g) raw shrimp, peeled, deveined and tails removed

1 tbsp (15 ml) avocado oil

½ tbsp (4 g) Meat Church Holy Voodoo seasoning (sub your favorite spicy seasoning)

2 large burrito-sized flour tortillas

1 large avocado, halved, peeled, and sliced

1 cup (113 g) Oaxaca cheese, shredded (sub your favorite melty cheese)

Spanish rice, for serving

Salsa, cilantro lime crema or guacamole, for serving

Blackened Mahi Mahi Tacos

Taco Tuesday took a turn for the coast! These mahi mahi fillets have an amazing non-fishy flavor and hearty texture with each bite. Combined with a crunchy and tangy slaw, they make for some amazingly easy and delicious tacos on the Blackstone!

MAKES 6–12 TACOS

Before starting on the fish, mix up a quick bowl of slaw to top the tacos. Add the tricolored coleslaw, mayonnaise, apple cider vinegar and Everything But The Bagel seasoning to a bowl. Mix it all up and let it sit in the fridge while making the tacos.

Bring your griddle up to medium-high heat.

Completely dry the mahi mahi off with paper towels. Then rub in a light coat of avocado oil and season all sides of each fillet with a light coat of the Meat Church Holy Voodoo seasoning (about ½ teaspoon on each side of each fillet). This method allows the fish to get a nice sear. If you put it down on the griddle wet, it boils rather than searing.

Place the fillets on the hot griddle and allow the first side to blacken for 2 to 3 minutes before flipping. You'll see the edges start to brown and blacken, which is your sign to flip the fillets. Cook the second side of the fillets for 2 to 3 minutes. Once they are close to being done, break them up with the spatula. Turn a side burner on low and slide the fish over there to stay warm.

Turn the entire griddle down to low and add your tortillas to the griddle top. After 30 seconds, flip the tortillas. Disperse the mahi mahi equally between the tortillas. Top the tacos with a large spoonful of the slaw, a sprinkle of cotija cheese and some chopped cilantro.

We served these up with some cilantro rice.

The combination of the super hearty and spicy blackened mahi mahi along with the tangy slaw makes for a great tasting taco!

SLAW

4 oz (113 g) tricolored coleslaw mix

¼ cup (60 ml) mayonnaise

1 tbsp (15 ml) apple cider vinegar

2 tsp (4 g) Everything But The Bagel seasoning

TACOS

4 (3–4-oz [84–113-g]) mahi mahi fillets

2 tsp (10 ml) avocado oil

4 tsp (10 g) Meat Church Holy Voodoo seasoning (sub your favorite Cajun seasoning)

6 soft taco–sized flour tortillas or 12 street taco–sized corn tortillas

¼ cup (60 ml) cotija or queso fresco cheese

½ cup (8 g) chopped cilantro

Cilantro rice, for serving

Beefy Cheesy Crunch Wrap Supreme®

I can always seem to wow my kids with a re-creation of some of their favorite fast-food orders. This copycat recipe from Taco Bell™ had everybody excited and tastes even better with quality ingredients and attention to detail. I have a feeling this dish will be on the regular rotation at your house after you give it a go!

MAKES 6 CRUNCH WRAPS

Set the lightly oiled griddle to medium-high heat. Brown the ground beef and onion for 6 to 8 minutes, until there is no pink remaining in the beef. Drain the grease into the rear grease trap. Stir the taco seasoning and water into the beef until combined. Continue to cook the beef until it starts to boil. Reduce the heat to medium and let the mixture simmer for 2 to 3 more minutes, stirring every minute or so. If your griddle has room, push the beef to the side. If not, remove it from the heat.

Warm the nacho cheese in a small pot on the Blackstone. Warm the flour tortillas on the griddle for 30 seconds per side. Place the tortillas in a tortilla warmer or between two plates to keep warm.

It's time to start building your crunch wraps. Lay one large flour tortilla on a flat surface. Spread ½ cup (118 ml) of taco meat onto the center of the tortilla. Spoon 2 tablespoons (30 ml) of nacho cheese over the meat. Top the meat with one tostada shell. Spread a thin layer of sour cream over the tostada shell. Top the tostada shell with a bit of lettuce, tomato and shredded Mexican cheese. Be careful not to overstuff these. Add the small street taco–sized flour tortilla in the center.

To fold the crunch wrap, start with the bottom of the flour tortilla and fold the edge up over the center. Continue to work your way around, folding the flour tortilla over the smaller, center tortilla.

Repeat with all the remaining tortillas, tostadas and fillings. You'll have 6 crunch wraps total.

Lightly oil your medium-heat griddle. Place as many crunch wraps as will fit seam-side down onto the griddle. Cook for 2 to 3 minutes, or until the tortilla is golden brown. Flip over and cook the other side until golden brown, 2 to 3 more minutes. Repeat this process with all the crunch wraps.

Serve them up with your favorite sides, like Mexican rice or charro beans and lime wedges.

1 lb (454 g) lean ground beef

1 medium white onion, chopped

2 tbsp (10 g) taco seasoning

¼ cup (60 ml) water

1 (15-oz [425-g]) jar nacho cheese or queso dip

6 burrito-sized flour tortillas

6 tostada shells (seasoned or unseasoned works)

1 cup (240 ml) sour cream

2 cups (140 g) shredded iceberg lettuce

1 large tomato, diced

1 cup (113 g) shredded Mexican cheese

6 small street taco–sized flour tortillas

Mexican rice or charro beans, for serving

Lime wedges, for serving

SUNDAY SUPPER

Of course, you could make these meals any day of the week, but there's something about having a little extra time to prep and cook on your days off. We enjoy having friends and family over and just being together around a great meal like the Reverse Seared NY Strip Steaks (page 56) or Southern Shrimp, Sausage & Grits (page 73). The thought of a recipe from this book helping bring people together absolutely makes my day! All the recipes here can be multiplied to feed a crowd or divided down for a single serving. As with all my recipes, I encourage you to tweak them and make them your own.

Reverse Seared NY Strip Steaks

The Blackstone is one of my favorites tools to use alongside my pellet grills. The reverse seared steak might just be the best example of what these two devices can do when working together. The introduction of wood-fired smoke flavor from the Traeger combined with the amazing searing capability of the Blackstone makes for an amazing steak that would rival any fancy steak house. This method can be translated to any other common steak cut of beef. If you find yourself without a pellet grill, you could always sear your steak on the Blackstone and then finish it off in the oven until it reaches your desired doneness.

MAKES 4 STEAKS

We'll start by setting our pellet grill to the lowest temp, 165°F (75°C), with the Super Smoke mode initiated, if available.

Season each steak with 2 teaspoons (5 g) of Meat Church Holy Cow seasoning on all sides. Add the steaks to the grill, preferably on a rack in the middle of the grill. Use an internal meat thermometer to track your temps.

After approximately 2½ hours, the steaks should be getting close to a 110°F (45°C) internal temperature. As they do, crank up your Blackstone to high heat. Make sure there is a light layer of oil over the whole surface of the griddle. We're looking for a surface temperature of 500°F (260°C).

Once the steaks hit an internal temperature of 110°F (45°C), remove them from the smoke and place them directly onto the blazing hot Blackstone. Flip the steaks every minute, until their internal temperature hits 135°F (60°C) degrees (medium rare). This should only take 2 to 3 minutes total.

Remove the steaks and top with pats of compound garlic butter. Let the steaks rest for 5 minutes or so, allowing the internal juices to settle down before slicing.

Serve these up with your favorite loaded baked potatoes or griddled veggies.

4 (12-oz [340-g]) New York strip steaks

8 tsp (20 g) Meat Church Holy Cow seasoning (sub your favorite steak seasoning)

4 tbsp (57 g) garlic compound butter

Loaded baked potatoes or griddled veggies, for serving

Tequila Lime Chicken Fajitas

Fajitas on the Blackstone . . . it doesn't get much better! This recipe was created by my buddy Matt Pittman and makes for some of the tastiest fajitas I've ever had. As soon as I saw it, I knew I had to tweak it to work on a Blackstone, and it had to be a part of this book. It requires an overnight marinade so make sure to plan accordingly—these are well worth the prep.

MAKES 4 SERVINGS

Start by mixing the olive oil, silver tequila, hot honey, lime zest, lime juice, jalapeño, garlic and Meat Church Gourmet Garlic and Herb seasoning together in a bowl. Add the chicken to the marinade and let it marinate in the fridge overnight.

The next day, set one side of your lightly oiled griddle to medium heat. Remove the chicken from the marinade and place it straight onto the griddle along with the julienned veggies.

Let the chicken cook for 3 to 4 minutes before flipping. Cook the other side for 3 to 4 minutes and then continuously flip every minute or so until the chicken reaches an internal temperature of 165°F (75°C), 8 to 10 minutes. Remove the chicken from the heat and let it rest for 5 to 10 minutes.

Remove the veggies once they get some color and start to soften, 5 to 6 minutes.

While the chicken rests, warm the flour tortillas on the griddle for 2 to 3 minutes per side. Slice the chicken and serve it on the tortillas with a mix of the sautéed veggies.

Serve these up with Spanish rice, black beans and your favorite salsa!

MARINADE

6 tbsp (90 ml) olive oil

6 tbsp (90 ml) silver tequila

2 tbsp (30 ml) hot honey

Zest of 2 limes

Juice of 1 lime

1 jalapeño, sliced

4 cloves garlic, grated

1 tbsp (7 g) Meat Church Gourmet Garlic and Herb seasoning (sub garlic salt)

FAJITAS

6 boneless, skinless chicken breasts

1 large white onion, julienned

1 green bell pepper, julienned

1 yellow bell pepper, julienned

1 red bell pepper, julienned

12 fajita-sized flour tortillas

Spanish rice and black beans, for serving

Salsa, for serving

Griddled Rib Eye Crostini with Horseradish Sauce

We host a lot of groups from our church, and I'm always looking for recipes like this to feed a lot of people. Featuring tender, juicy rib eye steak strips and a satisfying crunch from the baguette, this crostini recipe makes for a great appetizer or one course of many.

MAKES 20 CROSTINI

Bring the rib eye steak to room temperature while you prep the sauce and crostini. Place the sour cream, mayonnaise, horseradish, chives, Dijon mustard, salt and black pepper in a bowl and whisk together until well combined. Place in the refrigerator until needed.

Set your lightly oiled griddle to medium-high heat. Brush each slice of baguette with olive oil. Place the baguettes down on the griddle and cook each side for 2 to 4 minutes, until lightly golden brown. Remove them from the heat.

Turn your griddle up to high heat. Pat the steak dry with a paper towel. Season the steak with a pinch of salt and black pepper on both sides.

Add a tablespoon (15 ml) of olive oil to the griddle. Place the steak onto the blazing hot griddle. Use a burger press to press the steak down to ensure it touches the surface of the griddle. Cook for 2 minutes. Flip the steak and cook for 2 more minutes. Repeat this process, cooking for an additional 2 minutes per side, for a total of 8 minutes.

Remove the steak to a cutting board and make a loose foil tent over the top. Let it rest for 5 minutes. After the 5-minute rest, slice the steak into thin slices. You'll want to get at least 20 slices to top each slice of toasted baguette.

Top each baguette with a slice of steak and add a dollop of the Horseradish Sauce, a drizzle of balsamic glaze and a sprinkle of chopped chives. Plate these on a platter and watch them disappear!

1 boneless rib eye steak, ½" to 1" (1.3 to 2.5 cm) thick

HORSERADISH SAUCE

1 cup (240 ml) sour cream

2 tbsp (30 ml) mayonnaise

4 tbsp (60 ml) prepared horseradish

2 tbsp (6 g) finely chopped chives

2 tsp (10 ml) Dijon mustard

Pinch of salt and ground black pepper

CROSTINI

1 baguette, sliced into ½" (1.3-cm)-thick slices, approximately 20 slices

¼ cup (60 ml) extra virgin olive oil

Pinch of salt and ground black pepper

Balsamic glaze, for drizzling

2 tbsp (6 g) chopped chives, to garnish each rib eye crostini

Mayo-Marinated Chicken Breasts

Mayo marinated—yeah, you heard that one right. I probably had the same initial reaction to hearing that title for the first time. Blackstone Betty convinced me to try it, and I'm so glad I did. This process is super simple but makes for some of the tastiest and juiciest chicken you're ever going to get off the griddle!

MAKES 4 SERVINGS

Combine the mayonnaise and seasoning in a bowl until well mixed.

Add the chicken and seasoned mayonnaise to a large zip-top bag. Mix the contents, making sure the chicken is covered. Allow the chicken to marinate for at least 20 minutes or up to 4 hours.

When you're ready to cook the chicken, set your griddle to medium-low. The mayonnaise contains oil, so there is no need to add any additional oil to your griddle before cooking. Place the marinated chicken on the griddle top and allow it to cook for 4 to 5 minutes per side, or until golden brown. Remove the chicken from the griddle when the internal temperature reaches 165°F (75°C) at the thickest point of the breast.

Allow the chicken to rest for 2 to 3 minutes before slicing. Add it to your favorite salad, wraps or eat it with griddled veggies.

½ cup (120 ml) Duke's Mayonnaise (sub any non-vegan mayonnaise)

1 tbsp (5 g) Blackstone's Whiskey Burger seasoning (sub any all-purpose seasoning)

4 boneless skinless chicken breasts, trimmed of fat and gristle

Chicken Fried Steaks & Bacon Gravy

Growing up in Texas, I always thought that chicken fried steak was a staple in every American's home. It wasn't until I met my wife in high school that I realized not everyone has had the pleasure of trying this delicious and crispy take on steak. Let's change that. I can't wait for you to try this amazing southern staple, no matter where you're reading this book from.

MAKES 4 STEAKS

Start by making sure your steaks are all tenderized to an even thinness. If needed, use plastic wrap and a meat tenderizing mallet to pound them into submission. Lightly salt the steaks with a pinch of salt.

In a large, shallow bowl, mix the beaten eggs and buttermilk. This will be your wash.

In another large, shallow bowl, mix the flour, 2 teaspoons (12 g) of salt, garlic powder, black pepper, cayenne and Blackstone Breakfast Blend together until well combined. This will be the dredge.

Turn the middle two burners of the griddle to medium heat. Add the canola oil to the griddle.

As the griddle oil is coming up to heat, place a steak in the dredge (flour mix). Flip and make sure all sides of the steak have touched the flour. Remove the steak from the dry dredge and place it in the wash (egg mixture). Again, flip and make sure all sides get the wash adhered. Remove the steak from the wash and back into the dredge. Flip and push the steak down into the dredge to make sure all sides are coated well. You're looking for a thick coating here, so don't shake off any excess flour or egg mixture. Repeat this for each steak.

Once the griddle is up to temp, drop a small bit of flour in the oil. If the flour quickly burns, it's too hot. Turn the temperature down a bit and try again in a couple minutes. If the flour starts to fry right away, you are ready to go. Place each steak into the oil for a shallow fry. Leave them alone until you see the edges of the steak starting to brown, 3 to 4 minutes. Flip the steaks and cook for an additional 3 to 4 minutes, until the steaks are golden brown. Place the fried steaks on a warming rack off to the side of the griddle to stay warm while we make the gravy.

(continued)

CHICKEN FRIED STEAKS

1 lb (454 g) pre-tenderized cube steaks, or round steaks (4 steaks)

2 tsp (12 g) salt, plus more as needed

3 large eggs, beaten

1 cup (240 ml) buttermilk

2 cups (250 g) all-purpose flour

1½ tsp (7 g) garlic powder

1 tsp coarse ground black pepper

½ tsp cayenne

1 tsp Blackstone Breakfast Blend seasoning

1 cup (240 ml) canola oil

Chicken Fried Steaks & Bacon Gravy (continued)

Reserve 3 tablespoons (45 ml) of the cooking oil. Scrape and clean the griddle. Add a thin layer of fresh oil if needed to keep your griddle properly seasoned and protected.

Place a pot on the griddle over medium heat. Add the reserved cooking oil and 3 tablespoons (24 g) of flour to the pot. Whisk constantly and cook until it's the color of a light chocolate milk, 4 to 5 minutes. Slowly add the heavy cream to the pot, stirring continuously. Crumble the cooked bacon and add it to the pot. If the gravy is too thick, you can add a tablespoon (15 ml) of heavy cream at a time to thin it out. Once the gravy is to your desired thickness, add a pinch of salt, Breakfast Blend seasoning and a lot of coarse black pepper.

Serve up the fried steaks with mashed potatoes and gravy over everything. Garnish with chopped parsley and serve hot.

BACON GRAVY

3 tbsp (45 ml) reserved cooking oil (sub bacon grease if available)

3 tbsp (24 g) all-purpose flour

2 cups (480 ml) heavy cream, plus more as needed

4 slices cooked bacon (see page 118)

Kosher salt, to taste

1 tsp Blackstone Breakfast Blend

Freshly ground black pepper, to taste

2 lb (907 g) Bob Evans Mashed Potatoes, prepared per directions for serving

Parsley, chopped, for garnish

Blackened Salmon with Cajun Crawfish Sauce & Dirty Rice

I love crawfish! Fried, boiled or grilled, any way I can get them. As I started to widen my culinary horizons, I knew crawfish had to be included in as many recipes as possible. In this recipe, the creamy and rich sauce pairs perfectly with the blackened Cajun-seasoned salmon—and, of course, the dirty rice is there to catch any of the sauce that might make its way to the bottom of your plate. I guarantee you're going to love this dish!

MAKES 4 SERVINGS

Let's start by preparing the dirty rice mix per the box instructions. This can be accomplished on the Blackstone, or on a side burner. Before cooking, add the fire roasted diced tomatoes to the mix. We generally leave the optional added protein out.

Let's get to that sauce! Add 1 tablespoon (15 ml) of olive oil to a lightly oiled, medium-heat griddle. Once up to temp, sauté the shallots and onion for 2 to 3 minutes, until tender. Add the garlic and cook up until fragrant, about 30 seconds. Add the crawfish to the veggies and season with the Meat Church Holy Voodoo seasoning. Cook for 2 to 3 minutes, until the crawfish start to brown a bit, then reserve a few for garnish at the end.

(continued)

DIRTY RICE

8 oz (226 g) boxed dirty rice mix

1 (14-oz [392-g]) can fire roasted diced tomatoes, drained

CAJUN CRAWFISH SAUCE

2 tbsp (30 ml) olive oil, divided

3 tbsp (42 g) minced shallots, reserve 1 tbsp (14 g) for garnish

½ cup (80 g) diced yellow onion

1 tbsp (8 g) minced garlic

1 lb (454 g) crawfish tails, cooked and peeled

2 tsp (5 g) Meat Church Holy Voodoo seasoning (sub your favorite Cajun seasoning)

Blackened Salmon with Cajun Crawfish Sauce & Dirty Rice (continued)

Add a pot to the griddle and crank it up to medium-high heat. Place the remaining tablespoon (15 ml) of olive oil, the sautéed crawfish, veggies and butter in the pot. Once the butter starts to melt, slowly pour the heavy cream in while constantly stirring. Add the hot sauce and Worcestershire sauce. Bring the sauce to a low boil and cut the heat down to a low simmer. Stir frequently for 8 to 12 minutes, until the sauce thickens. Season with salt and black pepper to taste.

With the sauce set up, let's work on that salmon. Pat the salmon dry with paper towels. Drizzle each filet with 1 teaspoon of the avocado oil and apply a good coat of Meat Church Holy Voodoo seasoning. Place the salmon on a lightly oiled medium-heat griddle for approximately 5 minutes per side, until fully cooked through. The seasoning contains a bit of sugar, which will cause some blackening of the crust. That's all part of the plan.

Serve up this dish of dirty rice, blackened salmon and crawfish sauce. Garnish with the reserved green onions, reserved minced shallots and reserved sautéed crawfish. This is one heck of a Cajun meal that I know you will enjoy!

1 tbsp (14 g) unsalted butter

2 cups (480 ml) heavy cream

1 tbsp (15 ml) jalapeño hot sauce

1 tbsp (15 ml) Worcestershire sauce

Salt and ground black pepper, to taste

SALMON

4 (5-oz [141-g]) skinless salmon fillets

4 tsp (20 ml) avocado oil

4 tsp (10 g) Meat Church Holy Voodoo seasoning (sub your favorite Cajun seasoning)

¼ cup (12 g) chopped green onions, for garnish

Seared Scallops

Get your fancy pants on and griddle up a dish fit for a king. Scallops were always intimidating to me, but once we tackled them on the Blackstone, they were a breeze and turned out way more flavorful than expected. They work great as an appetizer, side or a main dish. Nail this recipe and impress all your griddle-envy friends at the next block party!

MAKES 4 SERVINGS

Let's start by patting the scallops dry with a paper towel. This will allow a good sear to occur. Season one side of the scallops with a pinch of salt and black pepper.

Turn your lightly oiled griddle to medium-high heat and add your olive oil. When hot, carefully place the scallops seasoned side down on the griddle. Allow them to cook undisturbed for approximately 2 minutes, or until the bottoms are browned.

Season the unseasoned side of the scallops with a pinch of salt and black pepper. Flip the scallops. If they stick, give them a side wiggle to help release them.

Immediately add the butter and garlic to the griddle top, among the scallops. Use a food safe silicone brush to brush the butter and garlic onto the scallops as they continue to cook another minute or two. Both sides should now be browned.

Remove the scallops and garlic and top with chopped basil and lemon slices. These go great served with an orzo rice pilaf.

1½ lb (680 g) large sea scallops

Pinch of salt and ground black pepper

2 tbsp (30 ml) olive oil (sub high-heat oil)

2 tbsp (28 g) unsalted butter

2 cloves garlic, minced

½ cup (12 g) fresh basil leaves, roughly chopped, for garnish

4 lemon slices, for serving

Southern Shrimp, Sausage & Grits

I don't think there's a meal I crave more than shrimp and grits. Those creamy, buttery, cheesy grits with some flavor-packed shrimp . . . boy I tell you what! I thought I'd kick them up a notch and add some hot link sausages to the mix, and I'm so glad I did. On a traditional outdoor grill, the natural juices from the proteins just fall away to burn up. Not so on a Blackstone. Everything cooks in its own juices and natural flavors, adding a more in-depth flavor to the shrimp and sausage in this dish.

MAKES 2 SERVINGS

Let's get the grits going. Bring the milk, water and salt to a boil in a medium pot on the griddle, set to high. Whisk in the polenta grits and reduce the heat to low. Cook slowly for about 30 minutes, stirring occasionally. Remove the grits from the heat, cover and let stand for 1 to 2 minutes.

When there's about 10 minutes left on the grits, turn another burner to medium-high heat. Once up to temp, add the sliced sausages and cook for 3 minutes or so, until both sides start to brown.

Add the shrimp to the cooking sausages and stir to combine. The shrimp will cook in the sausage grease, so no extra oil is needed. Add the Meat Church Holy Voodoo seasoning and remove from the heat when the shrimp turn from translucent to opaque, 2 to 3 minutes.

Add a portion of the grits to each bowl and top each with a tablespoon (14 g) of butter. Top both bowls with shrimp and sausages. Garnish the bowls with some chopped chives, Parmesan and hot sauce.

2 cups (480 ml) milk

2 cups (480 ml) water

1 tsp salt

1 cup (167 g) yellow corn polenta grits

½ lb (226 g) hot link sausages, sliced

½ lb (226 g) shrimp, deveined and peeled

2 tsp (5 g) Meat Church Holy Voodoo seasoning (sub your favorite Cajun seasoning)

2 tbsp (28 g) unsalted butter

1 bunch fresh chives, chopped, for garnish

¼ cup (25 g) grated Parmesan cheese, for garnish

Hot sauce, to taste

Surf 'n' Turf over Smashed Potatoes

This was a meal we put together while on vacation, and it was cooked up on my 22-inch (56-cm) Adventure Ready Blackstone. Due to the size of the griddle, this had to be cooked up in stages. The Blackstone takes potatoes to a whole new level when smashed. The crispy outer crust seals in the seasoning and makes for some of the tastiest potatoes you've ever had. Rib eye steaks are high in fat content which translates to delicious flavors when seared on your Blackstone. All that, combined with buttery shrimp, will make this one amazing surf 'n' turf griddled dish!

MAKES 2 SERVINGS

Leave the steaks out on the counter to come to room temperature. Once they do, pat them dry with a paper towel. Season the steaks with the Blackstone Steakhouse Seasoning Blend on all sides and let them sit at room temperature until it's time to sear.

Boil the potatoes in a large pot of water for about 15 minutes, until fork tender. This can be accomplished on the Blackstone set to high or on a side burner. Remove the potatoes from the water and set aside.

Set one side of your griddle to medium-high heat. Add 2 tablespoons (30 ml) of olive oil for the potatoes to this side of the griddle.

As the griddle warms, place the butter, rosemary, parsley, green onion, garlic paste, salt and black pepper into a small cast iron skillet or pot and place it on the Blackstone or a side burner at low heat until melted, 6 to 7 minutes. Stir until combined.

Add the boiled potatoes to the medium-high heat side of the Blackstone. Season with a couple shakes of the Blackstone Steakhouse Seasoning Blend and spoon a couple tablespoons (28 g) of the herbed butter over the potatoes. Use a spatula or burger smasher and mash the potatoes until flat. Use another spatula to scrape any stuck potatoes from the smasher. Griddle up the smashed potatoes until the edges start to brown, 5 to 6 minutes.

As the potatoes are cooking, add the broccolini nearby, still on the medium-high heat side of the Blackstone. Season with a pinch of salt and black pepper and allow them to cook until softened and the florets begin to sear, 4 to 5 minutes. Spoon a little of the butter over the broccolini just before removing.

Once cooked, slide the potatoes and broccolini over to the low or off side of the griddle to stay warm. Scrape up the griddle and add a light layer of oil for the steaks, 1 tablespoon (15 ml).

TURF

2 rib eye steaks

2 tbsp (10 g) Blackstone's Steakhouse Seasoning Blend (sub your favorite steak seasoning)

1 tbsp (15 ml) olive oil

SMASHED POTATOES

1 lb (454 g) petite medley potatoes

2 tbsp (30 ml) olive oil

Blackstone's Steakhouse Seasoning Blend (sub your favorite steak seasoning), to taste

HERBED GARLIC BUTTER

1 stick (114 g) unsalted butter

1 tbsp (2 g) chopped fresh rosemary

1 tbsp (4 g) chopped parsley

¼ cup (12 g) chopped green onion

1 tbsp (8 g) garlic paste

Pinch of salt and ground black pepper

Crank the griddle up to high. Once the oil starts to have small wisps of white smoke, add the steaks directly onto the griddle top. Allow them to sear for approximately 2 minutes, then flip and sear for an additional 2 minutes. Repeat this step, flipping every 60 seconds until the steak has reached your desired doneness, 5 to 6 minutes for medium rare, 130°F (55°C) internal temp.

Once done, allow the steaks to rest for 5 minutes. Turn the griddle down to medium-high heat and scrape it clean with a fresh light layer of oil.

Dry the shrimp with a paper towel. Add a tablespoon (15 ml) of oil and stir until they are all lightly oiled. Season with a couple shakes of the Steakhouse Seasoning Blend and toss until seasoned well. Add the shrimp to the medium-high heat side of the griddle, stirring frequently. Remove the shrimp when they are no longer translucent and are starting to brown, 2 to 3 minutes.

Split the potatoes, broccolini and shrimp between two plates. Slice the steak and add the slices to the top of the potatoes. Top the steak with the herbed butter.

Sit back and enjoy this ultimate Surf 'n' Turf meal created on the Blackstone!

SURF

1 bunch broccolini, washed and trimmed

Pinch of salt and ground black pepper

1 lb (454 g) shrimp, deveined, peeled and tails removed

1 tbsp (15 ml) olive oil

Blackstone's Steakhouse Seasoning Blend (sub your favorite steak seasoning), to taste

BLACKSTONE WAS MADE FOR BREAKFAST

I think if we took a poll, most people would say they started their Blackstone cooking journey with either a breakfast or a burger.

Breakfast on the Blackstone is amazing because, depending on the size of your griddle, you can have all kinds of items going at the same time with different temperatures zones. What used to take forever on a stove top can be finished in minutes on a griddle. This chapter includes some of our favorites like Melanie's Migas (page 90) and Brisket & Egg Breakfast Tacos (page 78). Being from Texas, you'll see some Tex-Mex inspiration in a lot of these dishes. I hope you enjoy making these as much as I do!

Brisket & Egg Breakfast Tacos

These hearty tacos combine three of my favorite things: tacos, breakfast and BBQ. Leftover brisket can be used in so many ways. The Blackstone is the perfect tool to bring it back to life as it cooks in its own rendered fats and seasonings, bringing out a depth of flavor you can't get on a traditional outdoor grill. As the brisket warms in this rendered fat, it creates a crispy texture on the exterior that tastes amazing. Combine that brisket with the other ingredients in this recipe and you will create a masterpiece!

MAKES 2 TACOS

Depending on the size of your Blackstone, you may be able to prepare all the main elements of this breakfast taco at the same time. To start, set the lightly oiled griddle to medium heat.

Chop the brisket up into small bite-sized pieces. Place the brisket on the griddle and give it a stir every minute or so. The brisket should be ready to go when warmed through, approximately 6 minutes.

Place the eggs and half-and-half in a bowl. Add a pinch of salt and black pepper. Scramble together.

On the opposite side of the griddle from the brisket, drop the heat to medium low. Add 1 tablespoon (14 g) of butter and allow it to melt. Spread the butter out with your spatula. Add your egg mixture, making sure to use your spatula as a bit of a dam to keep the eggs from running into the grease drain. Slowly and gently drag the eggs around on the griddle as they start to solidify. As the eggs get to your desired doneness, approximately 6 minutes, fold them on top of themselves and set aside on the griddle to stay warm.

As the eggs are cooking, warm the flour tortillas on the medium-heat side of the griddle for approximately 2 minutes per side.

Cut the heat and split the eggs and brisket between the two tortillas. Top the tacos with a sprinkle of cheese, a splash of hot sauce and a dash of parsley or cilantro.

2 oz (56 g) leftover smoked brisket

4 eggs

4 tsp (20 ml) half-and-half

Pinch of salt and ground black pepper

1 tbsp (14 g) unsalted butter

2 taco-sized flour tortillas

1 oz (28 g) shredded Mexican cheese, for serving

4 tsp (20 ml) hot sauce, for serving

1 tsp parsley or cilantro flakes, to garnish

Ham, Cheese & Spinach Omelet

It doesn't get much easier than a protein-packed omelet on the Blackstone. There are endless possibilities on what you can add, but I usually find that the fewer ingredients, the more the flavor of each shines through. The salty pork and sharp and tangy Colby Jack cheese meld together for a delicious bite. This recipe can be multiplied to feed a crowd. If the size of your Blackstone allows, you can even get multiple omelets cooking at the same time!

MAKES 1 OMELET

First things first, let's cook this omelet low and slow. Set your lightly oiled griddle to medium-low heat.

After about 5 minutes, add the diced ham to the griddle and stir for 4 to 5 minutes, or until it's warmed through and starting to brown. Add the spinach and give it a quick toss with the ham. Immediately slide the mixture over to the side of the griddle, as the spinach will wilt quickly.

Place the 8-inch (20-cm) omelet mold on the medium-low part of the griddle. Give the griddle and mold a good spray with canola or any other cooking oil to keep it from sticking. Add the butter to the griddle inside of the mold.

Add a pinch of salt and black pepper to the scrambled eggs and give it an additional stir. Pour the eggs into the mold slowly. Let them cook for about 2 minutes and add your ham and spinach mixture to one half of the omelet. Top the same half with the shredded cheese.

After approximately 5 minutes, when you see the egg starting to harden and slightly brown on the bottom, carefully remove the mold. You may need to use a rubber spatula to help release it from the sides.

Fold the omelet over on itself and flip until the cheese is melted and the egg is firm.

Serve with your favorite hot sauce or salsa.

½ cup (110 g) diced ham pieces

½ cup (15 g) baby spinach leaves

1 tbsp (14 g) unsalted butter

Pinch of salt and ground black pepper

3 large eggs, scrambled

¾ cup (84 g) shredded Colby Jack cheese

Hot sauce or salsa, for serving

EQUIPMENT

8-inch (20-cm) Pancake/Omelet Mold

Sausage, Egg & Cheese MakMuffins

My daughter's nickname is Mak, so that is why we call these the MakMuffins. These little breakfast sandwiches are super easy to griddle up with very limited ingredients. Any time we can re-create a fast-food recipe at home and make it even better, it's always a hit! The 36-inch (91-cm) Blackstone has plenty of space and different cooking zones that you can get it all griddled up in no time.

MAKES 4 BREAKFAST SANDWICHES

Start off by warming the Blackstone griddle up to medium heat on all burners. Add four silicone egg rings with a quick spray of canola oil to the griddle. Break one egg into each mold and give it a stir to scramble it. Season each egg with a pinch of salt and black pepper. After 3 to 4 minutes, you will see the egg starting to firm up on the top. Remove the mold and flip the egg over for another 2 minutes of cook time.

While the eggs are cooking, place the sausage patties directly on the griddle. Season each with a pinch of black pepper. Flip the sausages every minute until done, approximately 6 minutes total cook time.

While the sausage and eggs are cooking, toast the cut side of the English muffins on the griddle top. After approximately 3 minutes, they should be toasty.

Once everything is done, assemble the breakfast sandwiches with the English muffin bottom, egg, American cheese and sausage. Finish with the top bun and serve these quick and easy breakfast sandwiches up!

4 eggs

Salt and ground black pepper

4 (2-oz [56-g]) pre-formed sausage patties

4 English muffins, sliced

4 slices American cheese

SPECIAL EQUIPMENT

4 silicone egg rings

Chocolate Chip Brioche French Toast

The week of Thanksgiving we usually find ourselves making more breakfasts as the entire family is together and off work and school for the week. The requests always tend to be on the sweeter side. This breakfast still ranks at the top of my wife's all-time favorite meals I have created on the griddle. I'm sure the chocolate has something to do with that!

MAKES 8 SLICES

Start by setting your griddle to medium heat and applying a very light layer of oil. In a bowl, combine the cinnamon, nutmeg and sugar and set aside.

Melt the butter on the medium-heat griddle, spreading it out with a spatula, across your cooking surface.

Whisk together the cinnamon mixture, eggs, milk and vanilla and pour the mixture into a shallow container. Dip each slice of the chocolate chip brioche into the egg mixture.

Fry the slices on the buttered griddle, frequently flipping every minute or so until golden brown, approximately 6 minutes.

Serve the French toast with warm syrup, chocolate chips, sliced strawberries and a shake of powdered sugar.

1 tsp ground cinnamon

¼ tsp ground nutmeg

2 tbsp (30 g) sugar

4 tbsp (57 g) unsalted butter

4 large eggs

¼ cup (60 ml) milk

½ tsp vanilla extract

8 slices chocolate chip brioche bread (sub challah or white bread)

½ cup (120 ml) maple syrup, warmed, for serving

5 oz (141 g) semi-sweet chocolate chips, for serving

4 large strawberries, sliced, for serving

4 tbsp (30 g) powdered sugar, for serving

Chorizo & Egg Breakfast Burritos

I don't know about you, but seeing big, melty, cheesy burritos just makes me happy. There are so many directions you can take a burrito on the Blackstone: breakfast, lunch, dinner . . . even desert. We made these chorizo and egg breakfast burritos for dinner one night and loved the way they turned out. Chorizo is packed full of flavorful spices, which is why I love using it. Those compound flavors add so much depth to any meal.

MAKES 2 BURRITOS

Turn the lightly oiled griddle to medium. Remove the chorizo from the casing, if applicable, and place it on the griddle. Using a spatula, break up the chorizo and allow it to cook. Make sure to give it a stir every couple minutes. Cook for 6 to 7 minutes. Once you see the chorizo turn from an orange color to a dark brown all over, slide it off to the side to keep warm.

Add the julienned onion and bell peppers to the area where the leftover chorizo drippings are. Allow them to sauté for about 5 minutes.

Place the eggs and half-and-half in a bowl. Add a pinch of salt and black pepper. Scramble together.

On the opposite side of the griddle from the chorizo, drop the heat to medium low. Add the butter and allow it to melt. Spread it out with your spatula. Add your egg mixture, making sure to use your spatula as a bit of a dam to keep the eggs from running into the grease drain. Slowly and gently drag the eggs around on the griddle as they start to solidify. As the eggs get to your desired doneness, approximately 6 minutes, fold them on top of themselves and set aside on the griddle to stay warm.

Scrape off the center of your griddle set to medium heat and apply a fresh, very light layer of oil. Heat your tortillas for approximately 1 minute per side and remove.

On a side table, let's start to build your burrito! Layer ¼ cup (28 g) of the shredded cheese in the center of the burrito. Continue with half of the eggs, half of the chorizo and half of the sautéed veggies.

Channel your inner Chipotle™ burrito roller and get that burrito rolled up tight, making sure to fold the ends inward. Repeat for the second burrito.

Place the rolled burrito back onto the medium-high griddle, seam side down, and let it start to brown on both sides, approximately 3 minutes per side should suffice. Slice your burrito in half and dress the plate up with some cilantro lime crema or your favorite salsa.

12 oz (340 g) chorizo

½ medium white onion, julienned

½ green bell pepper, julienned

½ yellow bell pepper, julienned

4 eggs

4 tsp (20 ml) half-and-half

Salt and ground black pepper, divided

1 tbsp (14 g) unsalted butter

2 large (12-inch [30-cm]) burrito flour tortillas

½ cup (57 g) shredded Mexican cheese

3 tbsp (45 ml) cilantro lime crema sauce or salsa, for serving

INSTAGRAM TIP: After you slice the burrito, don't immediately pull it apart. Let it set together for a minute or two. The cheese will kind of meld back together in the center. Then when you pull it apart, you should get a nice photo worthy cheese pull!

Blackstone Buttermilk Pancakes

A piled high stack of buttermilk pancakes just makes me smile every time. When you see a melting pat of butter on top and maple syrup running down the sides, you know you are in for a delicious treat. Let's channel our inner short-order cook and make this delicious breakfast!

MAKES 4 SERVINGS

Whisk the flour, sugar, baking powder, baking soda and kosher salt together in a bowl. Create a well in the center of the dry ingredients and pour the buttermilk into the well and crack eggs into buttermilk. Pour the melted butter into the mixture. Starting in the center, whisk everything together moving toward the outside of the bowl, until all the ingredients are incorporated. Do not overbeat; some lumps are okay.

Let this mixture sit out covered on the counter at room temperature for approximately 30 minutes. This will allow the buttermilk to work its magic and result in fluffier pancakes.

As you approach the end of the 30-minute wait time, heat your griddle on low heat for about 5 minutes. Add 1 tablespoon (15 ml) of oil to the griddle. Turn the heat up to medium-low and using a measuring cup, ladle ⅓ cup (80 ml) of the batter onto the griddle. Depending on the size of your griddle repeat this step, making sure not to crowd the pancakes.

Keep an eye on them and flip the pancakes after bubbles rise to surface and bottoms brown, 2 to 4 minutes. Cook until the other sides are lightly browned, 1 to 2 minutes. Remove the pancakes to a warming rack set on the griddle to keep them warm until all the pancakes are cooked and you are ready to serve.

Stack them as high as you like and top with a pat of unsalted butter and warmed maple syrup.

2 cups (250 g) all-purpose flour

3 tbsp (45 g) sugar

1½ tsp (7 g) baking powder

1½ tsp (7 g) baking soda

1¼ tsp (7 g) kosher salt

2½ cups (600 ml) buttermilk

2 large eggs

3 tbsp (42 g) unsalted butter, melted, plus more for serving

4 tbsp (60 ml) vegetable or canola oil, for the griddle, divided

½ cup (120 ml) maple syrup, warmed, for serving

Melanie's Migas

I named this one after my wife Melanie. If migas are on the menu at a restaurant, she is more than likely ordering it . . . the veggie version of course. The added crunch of the tortilla strips give this dish a texture and flavor combo that's hard to beat.

MAKES 2 SERVINGS

Turn the lightly oiled griddle to medium. Remove the chorizo from the casing, if applicable, and place it on the griddle. Using a spatula, break up the chorizo and allow it to cook. Make sure to give it a stir every couple minutes. After 6 to 8 minutes, or when the chorizo is browned, slide the chorizo off to the side to keep warm.

Place the eggs and 2 tablespoons (30 ml) of the cilantro lime crema in a bowl. Add a pinch of salt and black pepper. Scramble together.

On the opposite side of the griddle from the chorizo, drop the heat to medium low. Add the butter and allow it to melt. Spread it out with your spatula. Add your egg mixture, making sure to use your spatula as a bit of a dam to keep the eggs from running into the grease drain. Slowly and gently drag the eggs around on the griddle as they start to solidify. Add most of the tortilla strips to the eggs, reserving some for a garnish at the end.

As the eggs get to your desired doneness, approximately 6 minutes or so, fold them on top of themselves and set aside on the griddle to stay warm. I like to go ahead and add the shredded cheese over the eggs at this stage to let it melt.

Place your flour or corn tortillas on the griddle and allow them to warm through, about a minute per side.

It's time to start building your migas! In a bowl, add half of the eggs, topped with half of the chorizo. Add half of the diced avocado, a spoonful of diced tomatoes (save the rest for another recipe), chopped cilantro, and top it all off with the reserved tortilla strips. Repeat for the second bowl and top both with a sprinkle of cotija cheese while doing your best Salt Bae impersonation.

Serve these up with a couple warm tortillas and your favorite salsa or hot sauce.

9 oz (255 g) chorizo (sub soyrizo for a vegetarian option)

6 large eggs

2 tbsp (30 ml) cilantro lime crema (sub half-and-half)

Pinch of salt and ground black pepper

1 tbsp (14 g) unsalted butter

1 oz (28 g) tortilla strips (sub lightly crushed tortilla chips)

3 oz (85 g) shredded Monterey Jack cheese

4 taco-sized flour or corn tortillas, for serving

1 large avocado, diced

1 (14-oz [392-g]) can fire roasted diced tomatoes, drained

1 bunch cilantro, chopped

1 tbsp (4 g) cotija cheese

Salsa or hot sauce, for serving

SERIOUSLY SPECTACULAR SANDWICHES

There are so many ways to make a great sandwich on the Blackstone!
The Blackstone allows you to prepare the whole thing right there in
one spot: toast your breads, warm up your meats and melt your cheeses
all on the same cooktop. Change up the protein, bread or toppings and
you can have a completely different flavor profile in the blink of an
eye. This chapter includes some classics, like Turkey & Ham Massive
Muffuletta (page 94) and Whatever You Call It Cheesesteaks
(page 98), and maybe some new sandwiches you've never thought
would be possible on a griddle, like the Nashville Hot Chicken
Sandwich (page 97). I can guarantee they all will leave your friends and
family wondering when they're going to get their Blackstone!

Turkey & Ham Massive Muffuletta

There's not a sandwich out there that gets my mouth watering like a good New Orleans–style muffuletta. That olive tapenade in combination with warm deli meats and melted cheese may just be the perfect combination, especially when griddled to perfection on the Blackstone. It's important to note that a traditional muffuletta uses a "muff" bun that can be hard to find in some areas. An Italian sourdough round is great substitution.

MAKES 4 SANDWICH QUARTERS

Let's start by heating your lightly oiled griddle up to medium heat. Slice your Italian sourdough round loaf in half, horizontally. Spread the mayonnaise on the cut side of the top and bottom bun. Place the mayo side of the bun onto the griddle top, and allow it to toast for approximately 5 minutes. Make sure to check every minute or so to make sure it doesn't burn.

As the bun is toasting, place the turkey and ham on the griddle to warm through and brown up just a bit.

Once the bun is toasted, place the bottom bun on a warming rack over the griddle. Stack your turkey and ham onto the bottom bun. Top evenly with the provolone cheese. Pour the water on the griddle and close the hood or dome to melt the cheese. After approximately 5 minutes the cheese should be melted. Top the melted provolone with a cup of the olive tapenade and add your top bun.

Remove the sandwich from the heat and slice it into your desired number of servings. We cut this big dude up into quarters and feed the whole family!

Italian sourdough round loaf

2 tbsp (30 ml) mayonnaise

2 oz (56 g) thinly sliced turkey breast

2 oz (56 g) thinly sliced smoked ham

6 slices provolone cheese

½ cup (120 ml) water

1 cup (60 g) olive tapenade

Nashville Hot Chicken Sandwich

I'm in love with all things Nashville Hot, and I don't care who knows it! Spicy, crispy and delicious . . . this sandwich fires on all cylinders. The addition of the pimento cheese mellows out the spice in the perfect way.

MAKES 4 SANDWICHES

Fill a large cast-iron pan half full of vegetable oil. Place the cast-iron pan on your well-oiled griddle on high heat. Heat the oil to 325°F (165°C).

Mix the flour and of Meat Church Holy Voodoo seasoning in a large shallow bowl for the dry dredge. In another large shallow bowl mix the eggs, buttermilk and hot sauce.

Dip each chicken thigh in the flour mixture first, making sure all sides are coated. Then dip into the egg mixture, covering all sides. Do one last dip into the dry dredge and then place the chicken into the hot oil. Allow the chicken to fry for 8 to 10 minutes, until the exterior is golden brown and the chicken reaches an internal temperature of 165°F (75°C). Repeat for each chicken thigh.

To make the spicy coating, in a separate bowl, mix the hot oil, cayenne pepper, brown sugar and Meat Church Holy Voodoo seasoning. Spoon this spicy coating over each piece of chicken to your desired level.

Build the sandwich on the hamburger buns with 4 slices of dill pickle, a fried chicken thigh, 1 ounce (28 g) of pimento cheese and a teaspoon of mayonnaise.

We served these up with some tater tot medallions cooked in the Blackstone air fryer.

FRIED CHICKEN

10 oz (283 g) flour

2 tbsp (14 g) Meat Church Holy Voodoo seasoning (sub your favorite Cajun seasoning)

2 large eggs

1 cup (240 ml) buttermilk

1 tbsp (15 ml) hot sauce

4 boneless skinless chicken thighs

SPICY COATING

½ cup (120 ml) hot frying oil (use this from your pan after you fry)

2 tbsp (11 g) cayenne pepper (adjust to your preference)

1 tbsp (14 g) brown sugar

1 tbsp (7 g) Meat Church Holy Voodoo seasoning (sub your favorite Cajun seasoning)

ASSEMBLING

4 hamburger buns

16 dill pickle slices

4 oz (113 g) pimento cheese

4 tsp (20 ml) mayonnaise

Tater tot medallions, for serving

Whatever You Call It Cheesesteaks

First off, I'm not even going to call this thing a "Philly." I'm not sure if there's a more highly coveted or contested food out there. Well, maybe the beans vs. no beans in chili debate. Whatever you want to call them, this hot, cheesy, 5-ingredient sandwich is a staple on the Blackstone!

MAKES 3 CHEESESTEAKS

Crank your Blackstone up to medium-high heat with a light layer of oil. As small white wisps start to come off the oil, you're ready to go.

Add your steak to the hot griddle. As the steak starts to sizzle, use two spatulas to separate the steak and chop it into smaller bite-sized pieces. The griddle top is tough and can take it. Once chopped up, allow the meat to sizzle for 30 seconds to a minute at a time before giving it a toss. Season the steak with 3 teaspoons (5 g) of the Blackstone Essential Blend, or your favorite SPG (salt-pepper-garlic) all-purpose seasoning. Toss it all up.

Shortly after adding the steak, place the sliced onion on the next medium-high burner over, making sure to give them a toss every minute or so. Add a teaspoon of the Blackstone Essential Blend to the onion.

After about 5 minutes, combine the steak and onion together. When another 4 to 5 minutes have passed, you should start seeing some searing action on both the steak and onion.

At this point, let's divide out the steak and onion slices into three piles, roughly the shape of your hoagie rolls. Top each of the piles of steak and onion with three slices of the white American cheese. I'm jealous of what you're about to eat right now! It's almost done!

When the cheese has been added, we're going to place a couple teaspoons (10 ml) of water on the griddle top, just a couple of inches from the steak, and close our hood or dome. This is going to help the cheese get all melty.

After a minute, let's remove the hood/dome and check out our cheesy masterpiece. If you need to go another minute to melt the cheese, go for it!

When the cheese has melted, we are going to open our hoagie rolls and place them face down on top of the cheesy piles of steak. Do this for each pile. We'll close the lid again and allow the buns to steam for another 1 to 2 minutes.

14 oz (392 g) shaved beef steak

4 tsp (6 g) Blackstone Essential Blend seasoning, divided (any salt, pepper and garlic seasoning will do)

1 medium white onion, sliced

9 slices white American cheese

3 Martin's Hoagie Rolls (I know I'm already in trouble for not using the right rolls)

Jalapeño kettle-cooked chips, for serving

When the buns have steamed and softened, slide a spatula under the whole pile, steak and all and give it a flip, with your hand supporting the top of the bun. You should be holding and looking at a gloriously messy creation of steaky goodness (I just made that word up). Plate your cheesesteak and repeat for the other two sandwiches.

Serve these up with some jalapeño kettle chips or whatever your heart desires

Be proud, you have made a cheesesteak!

Chicken, Bacon & Cheddar Bay Sandwiches

When I ordered up these Cheddar bay buns from Signature Baking, this sandwich immediately came to mind. This was inspired by Blackstone Betty's various creations and mayo-marinated chicken recipes. Thanks for the inspiration, Des! We made these sandwiches on our 22-inch (56-cm) Adventure Ready Blackstone on a trip to Clayton, Oklahoma. The views were breathtaking—but wait until you see the sandwich!

MAKES 4 SANDWICHES

Start by marinating the chicken breast cutlets in the pickle juice for about 2 hours. After 2 hours, completely dry the chicken off and add them to a bowl with the Chick-fil-A sauce, covering all sides of the chicken. Let the chicken marinate in the sauce as you prepare the rest of the sandwich.

Set your lightly oiled griddle to medium heat. Brush the Cheddar buns with a ½ tablespoon (7 g) of butter on each side and toast them up on the griddle. After approximately 5 minutes, the face of the buns should be toasted. Remove them from the heat.

Place the bacon on the griddle. Make sure to flip the bacon every minute or so until it reaches your desired doneness, 6 to 8 minutes. Also griddle up the sliced mushrooms, and season with salt and black pepper. Remove the mushrooms and bacon when done. Use a scraper to move most of the leftover bacon grease into the rear grease trap.

Remove the cutlets from the sauce marinade and shake off any extra marinade. Season each side of the cutlets with a teaspoon of Meat Church The Gospel seasoning and place them on the griddle top. Flip the cutlets every 2 minutes or so until they reach an internal temp of 165°F (75°C), 8 to 10 minutes total.

Once the chicken is close to done, top it with the mushrooms, bacon and Colby Jack cheese. Close the hood or dome for 1 to 2 minutes and allow the cheese to melt. Top the chicken with the chives and another shake of Meat Church The Gospel seasoning.

Plate these up on the Cheddar buns with lettuce, tomato, two pickle slices and plenty of Chick-fil-A sauce. The combo of the seasoning and Chick-fil-A sauce makes for some beautiful coloring and flavor!

4 chicken breast cutlets, pounded out (¼" [6-mm] thick)

3 cups (720 ml) pickle juice

3 tbsp (45 ml) Chick-fil-A® sauce, plus more for garnish

4 Cheddar buns

2 tbsp (28 g) unsalted butter

8 slices thick cut bacon

8 oz (226 g) sliced baby portabella mushrooms

Pinch of salt and ground black pepper

8 tsp (20 g) Meat Church The Gospel seasoning, divided, plus more for assembling (sub your favorite all-purpose seasoning)

4 slices Colby Jack cheese

1 tbsp (3 g) diced chives

4 lettuce leaves

1 tomato, sliced

8 pickle slices

Pico de Gallo Chicken Sandwich

I saw an ad for this Pico de Gallo Chicken Sandwich from Whataburger™ awhile back. They advertised it with grilled chicken, pico de gallo, pepper Jack cheese and a cilantro lime sauce. I thought, I can do that! Whoa, I'm glad I did! This sandwich turned out phenomenal—and it's even better because it was cooked on a Blackstone.

MAKES 2 SANDWICHES

Start by pounding the chicken breasts flat (you want them about ¼ inch [6 mm] thick) and seasoning both sides of each with 1 teaspoon of fajita seasoning. Put them on a medium-heat griddle with some light avocado oil and continued to flip until they hit 165°F (75°C) internal temperature, 8 to 10 minutes.

Slather 1 teaspoon of mayonnaise on each seeded brioche hamburger bun and griddle them up until they are toasty, approximately 4 minutes.

Place a slice of pepper Jack cheese on the bottom buns and pull your dome down to get it melty. After the cheese has melted, add the grilled chicken and top it with ¼ cup (45 g) of the pico de gallo, then top the pico with the cilantro lime crema and the top bun.

These were freaking amazing and looked way better than the ad I saw in the first place. Give this one a try!

2 boneless skinless chicken breasts

2 tsp (4 g) fajita seasoning

2 tsp (10 ml) mayonnaise

2 seeded brioche hamburger buns

2 slices pepper Jack cheese

½ cup (90 g) pico de gallo (see page 48)

2 tsp (10 ml) cilantro lime crema

Chopped Brisket Sandwich

Being from Texas, we love our brisket. Whether you smoke your own or stop by your favorite local BBQ spot, it's a great protein that just seems to spring back to life on the griddle top. As the brisket warms back up, the fat content renders, turning to beef tallow. The brisket literally cooks up in its own juices on the griddle, causing a flavor bomb explosion when added to your meals. These chopped brisket sandwiches are a quick and easy way to get that amazing low and slow flavor of your favorite hole-in-the-wall Texas BBQ shack in a meal right off your Blackstone Griddle.

MAKES 4 SANDWICHES

First, turn on the lightly oiled griddle and set all burners to medium-low heat (see Tip).

On one side of the griddle, place the leftover chopped brisket. If your brisket slices aren't already chopped, you can use a spatula on the cook top to chop them as they cook. That rolled cold steel can take it. Continuously stir the brisket as it begins to warm through.

Brush the inside of each bun, top and bottom, with about 1 teaspoon of mayonnaise. Place the mayo side of the bun face down on the griddle to toast it. After 3 to 5 minutes your buns should be golden brown. Make sure to check their progress every minute or so. Remove the buns from the heat and set aside.

As the brisket gets up to the desired warmth, 8 to 10 minutes, add the Sweet Baby Ray's to the brisket and give it a good mix on the griddle top. Make sure your heat is on medium-low. Higher temperatures can cause the sugars in the sauce to burn. Allow the mixture to warm and thicken for 1 to 2 minutes and then turn off all your burners.

Top each bottom bun with 1 cup (220 g) of chopped brisket. Add 4 to 6 dill pickle slices and several slices of white onion, both standard TX BBQ additions. Add your top bun and it's ready to serve.

We served these Chopped Brisket Sandwiches with some super crispy tater tots cooked on high for 15 minutes (give them a shake every 3 minutes) in the Blackstone Air fryer.

TIP: Don't be afraid to slow your cooks down by lowering the temperature a bit. You'll find your cooking experience and results much more enjoyable if things are moving at a slower pace.

4 cups (880 g) smoked chopped brisket

4 potato roll hamburger buns

8 tsp (40 ml) mayonnaise

½ cup (120 ml) Sweet Baby Ray's BBQ sauce (sub your favorite BBQ sauce)

16–24 dill pickle slices

1 small white onion, sliced

Tater tots, for serving

Griddled Mediterranean Steak Gyro

This quick marinated steak gyro is packed full of awesome flavors and textures that come together perfectly on the Blackstone. As the steak sears up on the griddle, the juices from the meat combine with the marinade and create a tasty crust. The veggies add a freshness and crunch to this gyro that puts it over the top.

MAKES 4 GYROS

Set your lightly oiled griddle to medium-high heat.

To create the marinade, whisk the olive oil, lemon juice, garlic, oregano, paprika, salt and a pinch of black pepper in a large bowl. Spoon 1 tablespoon (15 ml) of the marinade into a small bowl and mix in the yogurt and water.

Combine the julienned green bell pepper and onion in the large bowl with the marinade. Using a slotted spoon, remove the veggies from the bowl and set aside. Add the skirt steak to the marinade and toss until well combined. Let the steak rest in the marinade.

Place the bell peppers, onion and marinated steak on the griddle. Cook up the veggies for 3 to 4 minutes, until softened and seared. Sear the steak 4 to 8 minutes per side, until it reaches your desired doneness. Remove the steak and allow it to rest for 5 minutes.

Warm the pitas or naan on the griddle for 1 to 2 minutes per side, until they start to brown.

Once rested, slice the steak against the grain. Add steak, sautéed veggies, tomato, cucumber, yogurt sauce and micro greens to each pita/naan.

MARINADE

⅓ cup (80 ml) extra virgin olive oil

½ lemon, freshly juiced

3 cloves garlic, minced

1 tsp dried oregano

½ tsp paprika

1 tsp salt

Pinch of ground black pepper

½ cup (120 ml) 2% plain Greek yogurt

2 tbsp (30 ml) water

GYRO

1 green bell pepper, julienned

1 red onion, julienned

1 lb (454 g) skirt steak

4 pocketless pitas or naan bread

1 large ripe tomato, chopped

1 cucumber, sliced into thin half moons

1 bunch micro greens, roughly chopped

FLATTOP FLATBREADS & PIZZAS

My mind was blown the first time I saw CJ Frazier of the Blackstone Griddle Crew create a flatbread pizza on a griddle! I had no idea this was even a possibility. With a little ingenuity and some extra equipment, you too can create a pizza or flatbread masterpiece on your very own griddle. I have found these flatbreads are great for using leftover BBQ, veggies and toppings from other meals that are easy to throw together on a busy school night or for a party appetizer on the weekend. I have included some of my favorites in this chapter including the Fig & Prosciutto Flatbread Pizza (page 110) and the Big Mac'n Flatbread Pizza (page 114).

Fig & Prosciutto Flatbread Pizza

It doesn't get much easier than a flattop flatbread on the Blackstone. We love re-creating meals that we've had at some of our favorite restaurants. This one was inspired by our favorite pie at Sixty Vines™. The salty prosciutto combined with the sweet figs and hot honey make for an amazingly flavorful bite.

MAKES 2 FLATBREADS

Start by heating the griddle up to medium-high. With a very light layer of oil on the hot griddle, add the flatbreads and allow them to brown for approximately 3 minutes per side.

Once browned, remove the flatbreads from the heat. Apply ¼ cup (60 ml) of the Alfredo sauce to the top side of each flatbread and spread, leaving the edges clear. Apply ¼ cup (29 g) of the shredded mozzarella and top with 1 ounce (28 g) of the smoked prosciutto dispersed throughout the flatbread. Top the prosciutto with 2 tablespoons (13 g) of the grated Parmesan cheese. Place small, 1-teaspoon dollops of fig preserves around the top of each flatbread.

Place the flatbreads on a warming rack over the griddle, which will prevent the crust from burning while the toppings warm and the cheese melts. Add the water to the hot griddle to create steam and close your hood or dome for 6 to 8 minutes. Once your cheese is melted, remove the flatbreads.

Add 1 cup (20 g) of arugula to each flatbread and top with a 1-tablespoon (15-ml) drizzle of hot chili-infused honey. I like to add some additional grated Parmesan cheese and crushed red chili peppers flakes to mine. Slice and enjoy this wonderful combination of flavors!

1 (2-pack) premade artisan flatbreads

½ cup (120 ml) Alfredo sauce

½ cup (57 g) shredded mozzarella

2 oz (56 g) smoked prosciutto

¼ cup (25 g) grated Parmesan cheese, plus more for serving

4 tbsp (60 ml) fig preserves, divided

½ cup (120 ml) water

2 cups (40 g) arugula

2 tbsp (30 ml) hot honey

Crushed red pepper flakes, for serving

Perfect Pulled Pork Pizza

BBQ, pizza and the Blackstone . . . need I say more? Okay, I will! One of my family's favorite ways to use leftover BBQ is by making up some of these flatbread pizzas on the Blackstone. Since we're using a premade naan bread as our crust, we can pile it high with all our favorite toppings and don't have to worry about the crust not cooking properly.

MAKES 2 FLATBREAD PIZZAS

Let's start by heating your lightly oiled griddle to medium-high heat. When the griddle comes up to temp, place the pieces of naan down. Flip every 30 seconds or so, until you see the naan start to brown a bit, 2 to 3 minutes per side.

Once you've browned your naan, place them on a raised warming rack and cook them indirectly for the remainder of the cook.

Here's where I like to throw my leftover pulled pork onto the lightly oiled medium-high griddle. Continuously toss the pork and you'll see it start to come back to life. The pork will start to release moisture and the edges will get crisp after 4 to 5 minutes. About 3 minutes in, I like to season the pulled pork with a teaspoon or so of the BBQ seasoning it was originally cooked with. When you achieve your preferred level of crispness, cut your heat off on that burner, allowing the pork to stay warm with residual heat as you assemble your pizza.

Place 1 tablespoon (15 ml) of your favorite BBQ sauce on each naan and spread it out with a silicone brush, making sure to leave some room around the edges for your "pizza crust."

Top each sauced-up naan with about ½ ounce (14 g) of shredded mozzarella cheese. Place half of the rewarmed pulled pork onto each flatbread and spread it around.

Top the pork with the remaining 1 ounce (28 g) of shredded mozzarella. Give each pizza a ¼ teaspoon shake of the same BBQ seasoning and top with a dash of parsley flakes.

Now, we are going to get our dome or hood ready and place the water down on the griddle around the warming rack. Close the hood or place a dome over the pizzas. The heat from the griddle will steam the water, causing it to in turn melt the cheese. After about a minute, open the hood and check on your progress. If you feel the cheese isn't quite melted enough, you can repeat the steaming process again.

Remove the pizzas from the warming rack and cut into your desired size slices.

2 garlic naans

2 cups (498 g) leftover BBQ pulled pork

1 tsp BBQ seasoning, plus more for garnish

2 tbsp (30 ml) BBQ sauce, divided

2 oz (56 g) shredded mozzarella cheese, divided

¼ tsp parsley flakes

¼ cup (60 ml) water

Big Mac'n Flatbread Pizza

Pizza + Big Mac™ = all my childhood food fantasies come to life! This was a fun take on a classic. It has all the ingredients you've come to expect from the iconic burger in a fun fusion pizza, pulled together for perfection on your Blackstone. I'm Loving It (and you will too)!

MAKES 2 FLATBREAD PIZZAS

Let's get started by mixing the Duke's Mayonnaise, ketchup, sweet relish, mustard, onion powder and vinegar in a bowl until well combined. Transfer to a squeeze bottle and chill until ready to use.

Set your lightly oiled griddle to medium-high heat. Once up to temp, brown the lean ground beef, making sure to break it up into a small bits. Season with salt and black pepper. Cook for 7 to 8 minutes, until no pink is visible in the beef. Drain any grease and remove the beef from the heat.

Scrape, clean and re-oil the griddle. Add the flatbreads top-down and allow them to brown for 2 to 3 minutes. Flip and add a light sprinkling of toasted sesame seeds to the tops. We need to get this looking as authentic as possible. Let the bottom toast up a bit for 2 to 3 minutes and remove the flatbreads from the heat.

Top each flatbread with a drizzle of the Big Mac sauce, leaving a 1-inch (2.5-cm) area around the perimeter for the crust. Add a quarter of the browned beef to each flatbread. Add the half of the cheese slices to each flatbread and top with the remaining quarter of meat. Distribute half of the minced onion and pickle slices across each flatbread.

Place the flatbreads onto the warming rack over the medium-high griddle. Add the water to the griddle around the warming rack and close your hood or place a dome over the top. The steam created will help to melt the cheese in about 4 to 5 minutes. Once the cheese has melted, remove the flatbreads from the heat.

Sprinkle the shredded iceberg lettuce across both and drizzle with more of the Big Mac Sauce over the top. Slice and serve up hot!

BIG MAC SAUCE

1 cup (240 ml) Duke's Mayonnaise

¼ cup (60 ml) ketchup

¼ cup (60 g) sweet relish

1 tbsp (15 ml) yellow mustard

2 tbsp (14 g) onion powder

1 tsp vinegar

BIG MAC'N PIZZA

½ lb (226 g) lean ground beef

Pinch of salt and ground black pepper

1 (2-pack) premade artisan flatbreads

Toasted sesame seeds

8 slices American cheese, cut into quarters

1 small onion, minced

20 dill pickle slices

2 tbsp (30 ml) water

½ cup (35 g) shredded iceberg lettuce

Mini Naan Pepperoni Pizza Bites

This is a great recipe to get the kids involved in. These little zesty and cheesy pizza bites are great as an appetizer, party food or main course. We've cooked them up and enjoyed them while having a movie night a couple of times. This recipe calls for pepperoni, but like any pizza, make it your own and use whatever toppings and dipping sauces you like.

MAKES 15-20 MINI PIZZAS

Go ahead and turn one side of your lightly oiled Blackstone griddle to medium-high heat and the other side to medium. Place the pizza sauce in a pot and add it to the medium-high side of the griddle. We'll keep this going throughout the remainder of the cook. Make sure to give the sauce a stir every minute or so and adjust the heat as needed. Once it starts bubbling, turn the heat down to low.

Spread the olive oil out across the medium-heat side of the griddle. Place the mini naan pieces down and allow them to cook for 2 to 3 minutes per side, until they start to brown a bit. Remove the naan and add them to a warming rack.

Place the warming rack over a baking sheet, off the griddle, to catch any mess from the next step. Add a spoonful of the warmed pizza sauce to each piece of naan. Sprinkle some of the mozzarella cheese over each naan and add your desired amount of pepperoni. Carefully take the loaded warming rack off the baking sheet and place it directly on the griddle. Turn the griddle up to medium-high heat. Squirt the water onto the griddle, near the warming rack to cause it to steam. Close the hood or place a dome over the warming rack. This steam with help the cheese to melt.

Use a pair of tongs to remove the naan pizza bites from the warming rack when the cheese is melted, 3 to 4 minutes. Sprinkle with Italian seasoning. Place the pizza bites on a platter with a bowl of the warmed pizza sauce in the center for dipping. Serve warm.

24 oz (680 g) tomato pizza sauce

2 tbsp (30 ml) extra virgin olive oil

7 oz (200 g) Stonefire Naan Dippers (sub any mini naan)

16 oz (454 g) shredded mozzarella

4 oz (113 g) pepperoni

2 tbsp (30 ml) water

Italian seasoning, for garnish

Chicken, Bacon & Ranch Tortilla Pizzas

If you have a couple tortillas, of any size, in the pantry you can create all kinds of delicious griddle pizzas on the Blackstone. Switch up the sauces, cheeses, proteins and veggies and get creative. These cook up extremely fast and are a great way to get the whole family involved. Use a rotisserie chicken or make some of the Mayo-Marinated Chicken Breasts from page 63.

MAKES 2 PIZZAS

Let's start off with your Blackstone set to low heat. Add the bacon slices to the griddle and let these cook low and slow, flipping every minute or so. I have found this is the best way to get perfect bacon without burning it. After 8 to 10 minutes of flipping, remove the bacon once it's to your desired crispiness. They always continue to crisp up a bit once removed from the heat. Once cooled, crumble the bacon.

Scrape the griddle of any excess bacon grease and turn the griddle to medium-low heat. Place the tortillas on the griddle, flipping after 1 to 2 minutes.

Let's start building the pizzas! Spread ¼ cup (60 g) of the ranch on each tortilla, leaving a border about 1 inch (2.5 cm) from the edge dry to act as the crust. Top with chicken, red onion and bacon, and sprinkle with cheese.

If you have a warming rack, place the pizzas on the warming rack and crank the griddle up to medium-high heat. Closed the hood or dome the pizzas. Remove once the cheese has melted, about 5 minutes.

If you don't have a warming rack, turn the griddle down to low and close and cook until the cheese has melted, 7 to 10 minutes.

Garnish the pizzas with a sprinkle of chopped parsley and the remaining 4 tablespoons (60 g) of ranch and slice them up!

8 slices bacon

2 burrito-sized flour tortillas (sub low-carb tortillas)

½ cup (120 g) plus 4 tbsp (60 g) ranch dressing, divided

4 cups (880 g) shredded rotisserie chicken

½ red onion, thinly sliced

2 cups (226 g) shredded mozzarella cheese

Fresh parsley, chopped, for garnish

GRIDDLED PASTAS . . . YEAH YOU HEARD THAT RIGHT

Who would have ever thought you could create killer pasta dishes on the Blackstone? Well, you can! The Blackstone acts as one large "pot" where ingredients and flavors can be tossed together to meld into a delicious dish.

With some out-of-the-box thinking and great ingredients, you can whip up some amazing pasta on the Blackstone, like Ravioli with Sausage & Peppers (page 122) and Griddled Ziti (page 129). All of these dishes can be multiplied and made to feed a whole lot of people, just like Todd Toven does on the Griddle More Tour every summer. Let's get those spatulas ready and get to it!

Ravioli with Sausage & Peppers

We are always looking for quick weeknight meals on the Blackstone. Between sporting events, practices and youth group meetings, squeezing in a quick meal can sometimes be a challenge. This quick and simple pasta dish on the griddle is a surprisingly easy and delicious option for those busy nights or a weekend get-together with friends and family.

MAKES 4 SERVINGS

Start by bringing a large pot of water to a boil on the Blackstone set to high or on a side burner. Add a tablespoon (15 ml) of the olive oil to the water. Once at a rolling boil, add the ravioli and flash boil for approximately 2 minutes (or according to the package directions). Strain the ravioli and set aside.

Bring your lightly oiled Blackstone up to medium-high heat. Add the peppers and onion to the griddle. Toss the veggies for about 3 minutes, or until they start to soften. Add the sliced sausage to the griddle and cook for 5 to 6 minutes, until it is browned and no pink is visible.

Add the garlic to the mix and cook until fragrant, 1 to 2 minutes. Add the remaining 2 tablespoons (30 ml) of olive oil and the ravioli to the mix. Gently toss every minute or so and cook until the ravioli starts to brown, about 5 more minutes.

Shake up the Loaded Italian Sear and Serve sauce and add about half of the bottle to the mix. Add additional sauce if the pasta still looks dry. Give it all a toss and cook for another 2 to 3 minutes until well combined.

Remove everything from the griddle and pour it into a serving platter or large bowl. Top with parsley flakes and Parmesan cheese. Serve warm.

3 tbsp (45 ml) extra virgin olive oil, divided

20 oz (567 g) premade four-cheese ravioli

1 green bell pepper, julienned

1 red bell pepper, julienned

1 medium white or yellow onion, julienned

19 oz (538 g) sweet Italian sausage, sliced

2 cloves garlic, minced

1 (16-oz [473-ml]) bottle Blackstone's Loaded Italian Sear and Serve sauce

Pinch of parsley flakes, for serving

3 tbsp (20 g) grated Parmesan cheese, for serving

Tuscan Chicken Pasta

We can't talk about pasta on the Blackstone without mentioning Desirée Ruberti, also known as "Blackstone Betty." Betty is constantly pushing the boundaries of what people think can be cooked up on the Blackstone. Betty's Family Style Sunday meals are legendary, and she often brings her entire family out on her online videos and livestreams to cook along with her. This recipe is my homage to her and all her hard work as a part of the Blackstone Griddle Crew and for all #GriddleNation.

MAKES 4 TO 6 SERVINGS

Start out by bringing a large pot of salted water to a boil on the Blackstone set to high or on a side burner. Boil the pasta for 8 to 9 minutes until your desired tenderness (or according to the package directions). Strain and reserve 2 cups (480 ml) of the pasta water.

Set your griddle to medium-high heat, and lightly oil with 1 tablespoon (15 ml) of the olive oil. Season both sides of the chicken cutlets with the Blackstone Tutto Italiano seasoning. When the oil starts to have wisps of white smoke, add the chicken. Cook each side of the chicken for 3 to 4 minutes, until the internal temp hits 160°F (70°C). Remove the chicken from the griddle, allow it to rest for 5 minutes, then slice it into pasta-sized bites.

Add the remaining 1 tablespoon (15 ml) of oil to the medium-heat griddle top. Add the chopped onion and cook until it starts to become translucent and soft, 3 to 4 minutes. Add the minced garlic to the onion and cook until the garlic becomes fragrant, about 30 seconds. Combine the spinach and the jar of julienned sun-dried tomatoes with the onion mixture and toss frequently for 2 to 3 minutes, until the spinach starts to wilt.

Mix the cooked pasta and Alfredo sauce into the spinach mixture and stir until combined. Turn the griddle down to low and grate half of the Parmesan onto the pasta. Stir to combine.

Let the pasta simmer on the griddle for 4 to 5 minutes so all the flavors can meld together. Use some of the reserved pasta water if needed to thin the sauce out a bit.

Serve up hot with the desired amount of fresh grated Parmesan.

1 lb (454 g) penne rigate pasta

2 tbsp (30 ml) extra virgin olive oil, divided

1 lb (454 g) chicken breast cutlets, pounded flat (¼" [6-mm] thick)

1½ tbsp (8 g) Blackstone Tutto Italiano seasoning (sub your favorite Italian seasoning)

1 small white onion, finely chopped

3 cloves garlic, minced

5 cups (150 g) baby spinach

1 (8.5-oz [241-g]) jar sun-dried tomatoes in oil, julienned

15 oz (425 g) Alfredo sauce

8 oz (226 g) Parmesan cheese wedge, divided

Three Cheese Mushroom & Spinach Tortellini

My buddy Todd Toven over at Blackstone has made tortellini on the griddle, or as he calls it "Toddeloni," a world-famous dish! Much like the ravioli dish in this chapter, this is a quick and easy meal that can be taken in so many different culinary directions. Add or subtract what you like or with what you have on hand at home. You really can't go wrong. This version is meat-free and a great option for any vegetarians who may be visiting . . . or living with you.

MAKES 4 SERVINGS

Start by bringing a large pot of water to a boil on the Blackstone set to high or on a side burner. Add 1 tablespoon (15 ml) of olive oil to the water. Once at a rolling boil, add the tortellini and flash boil for approximately 2 minutes until your desired tenderness (or according to the package directions). Strain the tortellini and set aside.

Bring your lightly oiled Blackstone up to medium heat. Add the onion and mushrooms to the griddle. Toss them for about 3 minutes, or until they start to soften. Add the garlic to the mix and cook until fragrant, 1 to 2 minutes.

Add the remaining 2 tablespoons (30 ml) of olive oil and the tortellini to the mix. Gently toss every minute or so and cook until the pasta starts to brown and sear, about 5 minutes.

Shake up the Garlic Parmesan Sear and Serve sauce and add about half of the bottle to the mix. Add additional sauce if the pasta still looks dry. Add the spinach and give it all a toss, and cook for another 2 to 3 minutes.

Remove everything from the griddle and pour it into a serving platter or large bowl. Top with Parmesan cheese. Serve warm.

3 tbsp (45 ml) extra virgin olive oil, divided

20 oz (567 g) premade mixed-cheese tortellini

1 medium white or yellow onion, julienned

8 oz (226 g) baby portabella mushrooms, washed and sliced

2 cloves garlic, minced

1 (16-oz [473 ml]) bottle Blackstone Garlic Parmesan Sear and Serve sauce

2½ cups (75 g) baby spinach

3 tbsp (20 g) grated Parmesan cheese, for serving

Griddled Ziti

Baked ziti was one of my all-time favorite meals as a kid. This griddled up version is just as tasty, but a whole lot more fun to make on the Blackstone. Make this recipe your own by adding mushrooms, marinated artichokes or other veggies.

MAKES 4 SERVINGS

Start by bringing a large pot of water to a boil on the Blackstone or on a side burner. Cook the pasta according to the directions on the packaging, but just shy of the normal amount of time. About 8 minutes. Drain and set aside.

Turn your lightly oiled griddle to medium heat. Once up to temp, add the Italian sausage and cook up until no pink is visible, 7 to 8 minutes. Make sure to break the sausage up into small pieces.

Add the diced onion and bell pepper to the sausage and toss until the veggies start to soften and take on some color, 4 to 5 minutes.

Make a small well in the middle of the sausage mixture and add the minced garlic. Cook until the garlic becomes fragrant, about 30 seconds to 1 minute. Combine the sausage mixture and garlic together and season with Meat Church Garlic and Herb seasoning and crushed red pepper flakes, if using.

Turn all burners to low. Add the marinara sauce and cooked pasta to the sausage and gently toss until combined and the sauce begins to simmer, about 5 minutes.

Serve up the ziti with shredded Parmesan, freshly chopped basil and a side of garlic bread.

16 oz (454 g) ziti pasta

1 lb (454 g) ground Italian sausage

½ medium yellow onion, diced

1 green bell pepper, diced

2 cloves garlic, minced

1 tsp Meat Church Garlic and Herb seasoning (sub any Italian seasoning)

Pinch of crushed red pepper flakes, optional

32 oz (907 g) marinara pasta sauce

¾ cup (85 g) shredded Parmesan cheese, for serving

2 tbsp (3 g) fresh basil, chopped, for serving

Garlic bread, for serving

Shallow Fried Chicken Parmesan

I love chicken parm . . . It's one of my guilty pleasure orders at any Italian restaurant. I think it's the contrast of textures between the crispy chicken, the savory sauce and the melty cheese that gets me every time. This version uses some shallow frying techniques and was a crowd-pleaser at our home! If you prefer a much cheesier version, I don't blame you. Add the mozzarella to your heart's desire.

MAKES 4 SERVINGS

Let's start by pounding the chicken breasts flat (you want them about ¼ inch [6 mm] thick). This will help them cook more evenly on the griddle top. Season the chicken with a pinch of salt and black pepper on each side.

In a large shallow bowl, mix the pork panko, 2 ounces (56 g) of the Parmigiano Reggiano cheese and the Meat Church Garlic and Herb seasoning until well combined. This will act as the dry dredge. In a second large shallow bowl, scramble the eggs and water. This will act as the wet dredge.

Dip each flattened chicken breast in the wet dredge and flip, making sure all sides are covered. Place the wet-dredged chicken breast into the dry dredge, flipping to make sure all sides are covered. Repeat this step for each chicken breast.

Turn the griddle to medium-high heat. Add the canola oil to the center of the griddle top. This oil will be your frying oil. When you start to see white wisps of smoke coming from the oil, add the chicken breasts.

As the chicken cooks, place the spaghetti sauce in a pan and set it on the medium-high griddle. The sauce will warm through while the chicken cooks. Make sure to give it a stir every couple of minutes.

Allow each breast to cook for 6 to 8 minutes per side, or until the exterior is crispy and the chicken has reached an internal temp of 165°F (75°C). You may have to flip the chicken several times during this process. Once the chicken is ready, remove it from the heat and let it rest for a moment, then slice it.

It's time to plate your dish! Place 3 ounces (85 g) of cooked spaghetti on each plate. Top each serving with a ladle full of the spaghetti sauce followed by the sliced chicken Parmesan breast. Add another ladle full of sauce on top of the chicken. Top it all off with some freshly grated Parmigiano Reggiano.

Serve to your friends and family, and watch as they are blown away at the versatility of the Blackstone Griddle!

4 boneless skinless chicken breasts

Pinch of salt and ground black pepper

1¾ cups (170 g) pork panko or panko bread crumbs

3 oz (85 g) grated Parmigiano Reggiano cheese, divided

2 tsp (5 g) Meat Church Garlic and Herb seasoning (sub with garlic salt)

3 eggs

2 tbsp (30 ml) water

1 cup (240 ml) canola oil

24 oz (680 g) spaghetti sauce

12 oz (340 g) spaghetti noodles, cooked

FLATTOP FUSION STIR-FRIES, NOODLES & FRIED RICE

I had to include a chapter for some of my favorite Asian creations on the Blackstone. If you think of the griddle as a big flat wok, the possibilities are endless when it comes to delicious Asian-inspired dishes like Griddled Shrimp Pad Thai (page 138) and Bangin' Basil Pork over Jasmine Rice (page 145)! I have included some shortcuts that might feel like cheating, but will speed up your dinner prep. Don't stop at these recipes though. Get out there and create some amazing Asian fusion meals of your own and make sure to tag me @joshhunt_griddlin.

Simple Shrimp Fried Rice

There are a ton of fried rice recipes out there that take a couple days to prep. This is not one of them. I have found the quickest and tastiest version out there that uses a bunch of shortcuts and comes together in just minutes on your Blackstone! I know you're going love it!

MAKES 4 SERVINGS

Let's kick things off by setting your griddle to high and adding the cooking oil.

When the oil starts to smoke, add the two bags of fried rice. Give it a mix every 30 seconds. After 2 minutes, add the shrimp and broccoli slaw to the rice and combine.

Cook for an additional 3 minutes, stirring frequently. Add the tomatoes, green onions and Japanese BBQ sauce. Continuously stir until all the shrimp are fully cooked, 3 to 4 more minutes.

Garnish with a pinch of toasted sesame seeds and serve hot.

2 tbsp (30 ml) canola oil (sub any cooking oil)

2 (16-oz [454-g]) frozen bags vegetable fried rice (I use Trader Joe's™)

1 lb (454 g) raw, tail-off peeled shrimp

12 oz (340 g) broccoli slaw

4 roma tomatoes, quartered

½ cup (25 g) green onions, chopped

¼ cup (60 ml) Bachan's Japanese BBQ sauce (sub teriyaki sauce)

Toasted sesame seeds, for garnish

Fried Wonton & Ahi Tuna Nachos

This was a fun and rewarding recipe that pushed my culinary palate early on in my Blackstone journey. These fried wonton pieces are airy, super crunchy and strong enough to be loaded down, making for the perfect nacho chip. This dish is the prefect fusion of sushi and nachos, and I can't wait for you to give them a try!

MAKES 2 SERVINGS

Start by patting the tuna dry with a paper towel. Splash all sides of the tuna with soy sauce to help the seasoning to stick. Season the tuna on all sides with the Everything But The Bagel, about 2 tablespoons (5 g) for each fillet.

Place 2 tablespoons (30 ml) of the avocado oil on the hot griddle and spread it out. As soon as you start to see white wisps of smoke coming from the griddle, carefully add the tuna to the hot oil and sear each side for approximately 60 seconds. This is a quick sear for the exterior. The inside of the tuna should still be raw.

Remove the tuna from the griddle and cut the heat down to medium. Cut the tuna into 1-inch (2.5-cm) cubes. Place them in the fridge to chill.

When the grill has cooled a bit, add the remaining avocado oil to the griddle. Shallow-fry the halved wonton wrappers in the oil. Your griddle size will determine how many chips you'll be able to fry at a time. Flip the wonton chips every 30 seconds or so, until they turn golden brown, 3 to 4 minutes total. When browned, place the wonton chips on a paper towel–lined plate. Repeat until you have 24 fried wonton chips, 12 chips per serving. As the chips are frying, add the sliced jalapeños on the side of the griddle and sauté for about 2 minutes, until softened and browed, and remove from heat.

Divide the wonton chips between two plates and add the chilled seared tuna. Top with the jalapeño slices, a drizzle of Japanese mayonnaise, several dollops of squeezable guacamole and a sprinkle of chopped cilantro.

Serve with sriracha and soy sauce and dive in!

2 (6-oz [170-g]) sushi-grade ahi tuna fillets

2 tbsp (30 ml) soy sauce, plus more for serving

4 tbsp (10 g) Everything But The Bagel seasoning

1 cup (240 ml) avocado oil, divided

12 oz (340 g) wonton wrappers, diagonally cut in half

2 jalapeños, sliced

Squeezable Japanese mayonnaise

Squeezable guacamole

½ cup (8 g) chopped cilantro

Sriracha, for serving

Griddled Shrimp Pad Thai

This dish is inspired by the great Chef Jet Tila's recipe from his cookbook *101 Thai Dishes You Need to Cook Before You Die*. Chef Tila is one of my favorite celebrity chefs who you can find all over the Food Network.

I get so much satisfaction making these kinds of meals on the griddle, the type of meals you would normally think would not work on a flattop. When we discovered griddled pad Thai, we knew we had discovered a winner! This one has become a regular around our house. Once you have tried it, I guarantee you'll be ordering a lot less takeout!

MAKES 4 SERVINGS

Let's start by soaking your dry rice noodles in hot water for an hour ahead of time. This will loosen the noodles as they start to soak up the water. After an hour of soaking, make sure to drain the noodles well, reserving a cup (240 ml) of the water. If you found fresh rice noodles you can just jump right on to the next step.

For the sauce, combine the fish sauce, white sugar, tamarind concentrate, fresh lime juice and rice vinegar in a bowl. Whisk together until the sugar has dissolved into the mixture. Set this to the side until later.

Go ahead and crank your griddle up to high. I made this on a 36-inch (91-cm) Blackstone, so I turned three zones to high, leaving a side burner off to place items as to not burn them. Once the griddle heat is up to high add 2 tablespoons (30 ml) of your avocado oil and spread it out a bit with your spatula.

When your oil starts to have wisps of white smoke it's ready. Add your garlic and continuously stir it until fragrant, about 15 seconds. Add the radish, shrimp powder and diced tofu and stir for a minute.

This is where I push these ingredients off to the side of the griddle that is turned off. Add the remaining 2 tablespoons (30 ml) of avocado oil to the hot side of the griddle. Once you see the white wisps again add the eggs to the griddle. Break the yolks and allow the eggs to fry. After 30 seconds, fold the eggs into the rest of the mixture on the cold side of the griddle.

Let's add the shrimp to the hot griddle, stirring for 30 seconds to a minute. As the shrimp begin to change color, mix everything together back on the hot side of the griddle for 3 to 5 minutes, or until the shrimp are pink and have begun to curl.

NOODLES

6–8 cups (620–960 g) medium rice stick noodles (sub fresh rice noodles)

SAUCE

½ cup (120 ml) fish sauce

½ cup (120 g) white sugar

6 tbsp (90 ml) tamarind concentrate

2 tbsp (30 ml) fresh lime juice

2 tbsp (30 ml) rice vinegar

PAD THAI

4 tbsp (60 ml) avocado or canola cooking oil, divided

4 cloves garlic, minced

4 tbsp (30 g) shredded sweetened radish

2 tsp (4 g) shrimp powder with chili

1 cup (250 g) baked tofu, diced small

4 eggs

20 large to medium shrimp, raw, peeled and deveined

Add the soaked or fresh noodles. Stir everything together and allow the pad Thai to cook for 3 to 4 minutes. The noodles will start to soften. At this point, we'll slowly add the sauce you mixed up plus the paprika. If you pour the sauce too fast, it may not give the noodles time to soak it up and may run into the grease trap. Add the sauce slowly with your paprika and continue to stir for 3 minutes or so, until the paprika is evenly distributed and the noodles start to soak up the sauce.

Stir in half of the scallions and half of the chopped peanuts. Mix well and cut the heat off on your griddle.

Divide the pad Thai between four plates and garnish with more scallions, chopped peanuts and bean sprouts. A fresh squeeze of lime just before eating is a great addition.

You can add chili paste or sriracha after or during the griddling process to add additional spice to this dish.

2 tbsp (14 g) smoked paprika, for color

6 scallions, julienned, divided

½ cup (73 g) chopped dry-roasted unsalted peanuts, divided

2 cups (90 g) bean sprouts, for garnish

1 lime, for garnish, optional

Chili paste or sriracha, for serving, optional

Bulgogi Udon Noodle Bowls

Wow! I even surprised myself with just how easy and delicious this recipe was. The process of marinating the beef and veggies ahead of time made mealtime so easy to throw together on a busy weeknight—and cooking these up on the Blackstone makes it even easier. The udon noodles just soak up all that flavor from the marinade and every bite is fantastic!

MAKES 2 SERVINGS

First, stir the soy sauce, sesame oil, mirin, brown sugar, honey, garlic and black pepper together in a bowl.

In a large zip-top bag, place the sliced beef, onion, carrot, mushrooms and green onions. Pour the marinade on top. Mix and set aside for at least 20 minutes or up to overnight in the refrigerator. When you're ready to start cooking, let the marinade bag sit out on the counter for 10 minutes or so. This step is important, as pouring cold liquid onto a hot griddle can cause it to warp.

Add the oil to the griddle over medium-high heat. Once your griddle is up to temperature, add the marinated bulgogi mixture slowly. Allow the bulgogi mixture to cook for 3 to 4 minutes, until the vegetables are tender and the beef is browned.

Add the udon noodles and oyster sauce. Stir-fry everything together for 2 to 3 minutes.

Separate the noodle mixture into two bowls. Garnish with a sprinkle of toasted sesame seeds and thinly sliced green onion.

BULGOGI MARINADE

4 tbsp (60 ml) soy sauce

1 tbsp (15 ml) sesame oil

2 tbsp (30 ml) mirin

1 tbsp (14 g) brown sugar

1 tbsp (15 ml) honey

6 cloves minced garlic

Pinch of ground black pepper

BULGOGI BEEF

11 oz (300 g) sliced beef rib eye

½ medium onion, sliced

½ cup (67 g) julienned carrot

½ cup (40 g) shiitake mushrooms, sliced

2 green onions, chopped

NOODLES

2 tbsp (30 ml) vegetable oil

2 (14-oz [392-g]) packs udon noodles

1 tbsp (15 ml) oyster sauce

Pinch of toasted sesame seeds, for garnish

1 thinly sliced green onion, for garnish

Japanese Okonomiyaki with Smoked Salmon

Welcome to Japanese-inspired night at our house! *Okonomiyaki* means "grilled as you like it." You can include all kinds of different vegetables, meats and seasonings in this dish. For my version of this Japanese dish, I went with traditional ingredients with the addition of smoked salmon. It's then cooked up like a pancake and will take your tastebuds on an international journey!

MAKES 2 OKONOMIYAKI

Mix the cabbage, scallions, panko, salt and eggs together in a large bowl and combine.

Place half of the mixture on one well-oiled medium-heat griddle in the size and shape of a large pancake, then repeat this process on a second medium-heat griddle. Allow the okonomiyaki to brown on both sides, 5 to 6 minutes per side, then remove from the heat.

Once removed, top with Japanese mayonnaise, sriracha, sesame seeds and furikake. Top with 2 ounces (56 g) of smoked salmon (sushi-grade poke salmon would be amazing on this as well).

3 packed cups (210 g) finely shredded cabbage

1¼ cups (62 g) chopped scallions, about 1 bunch

1 cup (56 g) panko bread-crumbs

¾ tsp sea salt

3 eggs, beaten

1 tbsp (15 ml) Japanese mayonnaise, for topping

Sriracha, to taste, for topping

Sesame seeds and Japanese furikake, for topping

4 oz (113 g) smoked salmon, divided, for topping

Bangin' Basil Pork over Jasmine Rice

Here we have another recipe inspired by Chef Jet Tila! This dish comes together in a flash and just works perfectly on the Blackstone. Spicy and sweet, this meal will have every taste bud on your tongue dancing! The addition of the fried eggs is music to my yolk-loving heart, so crank that griddle to high and get after it!

MAKES 4 SERVINGS

Bring your lightly oiled griddle to high heat. Add the canola oil and spread it out with your spatula. Once the griddle is up to high, add the ground pork, spreading it out over the cooking surface. Let the pork cook for about 2 minutes without touching it. After 2 minutes or so, slide your spatula under the pork and give it a flip and allow the meat to cook for another 2 minutes. Then break the pork apart into bite-sized portions.

Mix the garlic, Thai chilies, black pepper and green beans into the pork. Cook for 2 to 3 minutes, stirring frequently, until the green beans start to char a bit.

Slowly add the chicken stock, using the spatula to lightly scrape up any bits of stuck pork or garlic from the griddle. You may also need to use your spatula to keep the stock from running into the rear grease trap. You'll see the chicken stock start to boil and then reduce. Continue to stir every 30 seconds or so, until the stock reduces by half.

Add the Bachan's Japanese BBQ sauce and combine well. As the sauce combines with the stock, it will start to thicken.

Fry the eggs separately on another part of the griddle, set to medium heat. Set the fried eggs aside as the sauce thickens.

Add the Thai sweet basil leaves to the thickening sauce for the last 30 seconds.

Serve the Bangin' Basil Pork over the top of some jasmine rice and top each serving with a fried egg.

3 tbsp (45 ml) canola oil (sub other high-temperature cooking oil)

16 oz (454 g) ground pork

4 cloves garlic, minced

2–4 fresh Thai chilies, minced

1 tsp ground black pepper

2 cups (220 g) green beans, cut into small pieces

1 cup (240 ml) chicken stock

¼ cup (60 ml) Bachan's Japanese BBQ sauce (sub your favorite Japanese sauce)

4 large eggs

2 cups (48 g) whole Thai sweet basil leaves, loosely packed

Cooked jasmine rice, for serving

Poppin' Pepper Steak Stir-Fry

You'll know why I call this Poppin' Pepper Steak Stir-Fry when you start griddling this one up. This is a hot and fast recipe that is perfect for a blazing hot Blackstone. As with all my recipes, you want to make sure all your ingredients are prepped and ready to go before you start. There's not going to be a bunch of extra time to slice the steak once this gets going.

Pepper steak was always my go-to order as a kid. I loved the flavors, but I also loved how the larger pieces of steak and peppers made it easier to learn to use chopsticks. If you didn't grow up using chopsticks that frequently, then I challenge you to at least attempt to eat this recipe with them. I know you can do it.

MAKES 4 SERVINGS

First, set your griddle to high heat and add a teaspoon of oil.

Add the green and red bell peppers. Give the peppers a stir every 30 seconds or so. After 3 to 4 minutes the peppers should start to get tender. Remove them from the griddle.

Season your sliced steak with a pinch of salt and black pepper. Add the rest of the oil to the griddle top. Place the steak on the griddle and give it a stir every 30 seconds or so, giving the griddle time to leave some sear marks on the steak. After 5 to 6 minutes, the steak should be lightly browned.

Add the garlic and ginger to the steak and continuously stir, until it becomes fragrant, about 30 seconds. Add the peppers back onto the griddle and combine them with the steak.

In a bowl, whisk the soy sauce, sugar, cornstarch and water together. Add the sauce to the peppers and steak. Continuously stir and allow everything to cook for 2 to 3 minutes, until the sauce starts to thicken. Remove everything from the griddle top.

Serve over the top of white or brown rice.

1 tbsp (15 ml) canola oil, divided

1 green bell pepper, julienned

1 red bell pepper, julienned

1½ lb (680 g) flank or sirloin steak, thinly sliced

Pinch of salt and ground black pepper

2 tsp (4 g) minced garlic

1 tsp minced ginger

¼ cup (60 ml) soy sauce

1½ tbsp (22 g) sugar

1½ tbsp (12 g) cornstarch

¼ cup (60 ml) water

Cooked white or brown rice

TO-DIE-FOR DESSERTS

This has got to be my family's favorite chapter. We have some serious sweet tooths over here in need of an intervention. They were eagerly ready to do their duty and taste test all these desserts for y'all! You might be surprised to hear that you can make dessert on your Blackstone, but it's so easy to whip up exciting twists on family favorites like Sopapilla S'mores Quesadillas (page 150) Smashed Cinnamon Rolls with Pecan Icing (page 154), and Griddled Chocolate-Filled Cinnamon Toast (page 158).

Let's wrap this book up with some to-die-for desserts created on the Blackstone!

Sopapilla S'mores Quesadillas

This is an awesome, quick dessert recipe that you can throw together for any last-minute backyard get-together or campsite hangout. Making this dessert on the Blackstone gives you all the flavors of s'mores without the dangers of flaming marshmallows flying through the campsite.

MAKES 4 S'MORES QUESADILLAS

Start by setting your lightly oiled Blackstone griddle to medium-low heat. The size of your griddle will determine how many of these you can have going at the same time.

Combine the sugar and cinnamon in a shallow pan that will fit the tortilla when folded in half.

Brush some of the melted butter on one side of the tortilla and place the buttered side down on the griddle. Layer on your desired number of marshmallows, chocolate chips and a sprinkle of the crushed graham crackers on one half of the tortilla.

Fold the tortilla over and give it a flip every 30 seconds or so, until the chocolate and marshmallows are melted, about 2 to 3 minutes.

Remove the "quesadilla" from the heat and brush both sides with additional melted butter. Place the buttered quesadilla in the cinnamon sugar tray and flip, dusting the outside. Repeat for each quesadilla.

Slice each sopapilla s'mores quesadilla into four triangles and serve them up around the campfire or patio table and watch these delicious treats disappear!

1 cup (200 g) granulated sugar

4 tbsp (32 g) ground cinnamon

4 tbsp (57 g) unsalted butter, melted, divided

4 burrito-sized flour tortillas

1 lb (454 g) miniature marshmallows

12 oz (340 g) semi-sweet chocolate chips

4 (14 g) sheets graham crackers, crushed into chunks

Griddled Peaches with Brown Butter & Cinnamon Toast Brioche Crumbs

I had to bring this one back for this book. This was one of my entries for the Blackstone Great Griddle Off contest back in 2020. This recipe and photo helped to push me forward in the competition, where I ended up winning the Golden Spatula award.

MAKES 4 SERVINGS

To make the cinnamon toast crumbs, preheat the oven to 350°F (175°C). Line a baking sheet with parchment paper and add the breadcrumbs, melted butter and cinnamon sugar. Toss everything together, coating the crumbs. Transfer the sheet to the oven and bake the brioche crumbs for 10 to 15 minutes, until toasted.

To make the brown butter, place the butter in a skillet set over medium heat on the Blackstone. Allow the butter to brown until it smells toasted and is a deep golden brown, 3 to 4 minutes. Stir often. Remove the butter from the heat and transfer it to a heat-proof bowl. Stir in the honey, vanilla and cinnamon. The butter can be used immediately or cooled completely and stored for up to 1 week in the fridge. Bring the brown butter to room temperature before serving.

For the peaches, set the lightly oiled griddle to medium-high heat. Add the peaches, cut side down. Griddle until heated throughout and caramelized, 6 to 7 minutes.

Serve the peaches topped with vanilla ice cream, brown butter and cinnamon toast brioche crumbs.

CINNAMON TOAST CRUNCH BRIOCHE CRUMB

4 slices brioche bread, torn or pulsed into fine crumbs (about 2 cups [216 g] of crumbs)

4 tbsp (57 g) salted butter, melted

4 tbsp (60 g) cinnamon sugar

BROWN BUTTER

4 tbsp (57 g) salted butter

2 tbsp (30 ml) honey

1 tsp vanilla extract

½ tsp ground cinnamon

GRIDDLED PEACHES

2 peaches, halved, peeled and pits removed

1 pint (473 ml) vanilla ice cream, for serving

Smashed Cinnamon Rolls with Pecan Icing

As far as desserts on the griddle go, it doesn't get much easier than these smashed cinnamon rolls. Smashing them flat allows them to cook evenly on the griddle and gives them a nice crispy finish. They are great for an after dinner sweet treat or as a campsite breakfast.

MAKES 10 SMASHED CINNAMON ROLLS

Turn your lightly oiled griddle to medium heat. Remove the cinnamon rolls from the packaging and separate them from each other. Place the supplied icing on the counter to soften.

The size of your griddle will dictate how many cinnamon rolls you can make at a time. You'll want to leave room to smash the rolls, without them touching each other, as well as a spot for the pecans to cook up. I prepared these on the 36-inch (91-cm) model and had plenty of room for everything at once.

Add half of the cinnamon butter to the griddle top and spread it out with a spatula. Place the cinnamon rolls on the buttered griddle, flat sides down. Smash each cinnamon roll down flat, using parchment paper to keep the cinnamon rolls from sticking to your burger smasher (you may need a bit of butter on the parchment paper to keep it from sticking as well). Once they are all smashed flat allow them to cook until the bottom is golden brown, 2 to 3 minutes. Flip them when golden brown and allow the other side to come to a golden brown color as well, another 2 to 3 minutes.

As the cinnamon rolls are cooking, add the remaining butter to the griddle and add the chopped pecans. Give them a stir every minute or so. Remove when they are warmed through and the cinnamon rolls are ready.

Allow the smashed cinnamon rolls to cool for about 2 minutes. As they do, stir the icing and warm pecans together in a bowl until combined.

Serve up the cinnamon rolls with the pecan icing drizzled over the top!

2 (17.5-oz [496-g]) cans Pillsbury Grands! Cinnamon Rolls with Cinnabon Cinnamon and Original Icing (sub any other canned cinnamon rolls)

6 tbsp (85 g) cinnamon compound butter, divided (sub plain, unsalted butter)

½ cup (55 g) chopped pecans

Strawberry, Lemon & Brie Grilled Cheese

The Blackstone Griddle is the ultimate grilled cheese making device, so why not make grilled cheese for dessert? These sweet and cheesy dessert sandwiches can be enjoyed any time of the day. The sweetness of the strawberries and sour lemon complement each other well as they meld with the savory melted brie!

MAKES 4 SANDWICHES

Let's start by bringing your lightly oiled griddle to medium-high heat. Once up to temp, add the chopped strawberries to the griddle and let them cook for about 1 minute before giving them a toss. Allow the strawberries to cook another minute, and then move them to a mixing bowl. Scrape up anything left behind and keep the griddle on medium-high heat.

Add the basil, olive oil, balsamic vinegar, lemon zest and a pinch of salt and black pepper to the strawberries in the mixing bowl. Stir until well combined.

Butter one side of each slice of sourdough. Slice the brie cheese into quarters.

Add 4 of the sourdough slices to the hot griddle, buttered side down. Top each slice of sourdough with a quarter of the strawberry mixture and a quarter of the Brie. Top each with a slice of sourdough, buttered side up.

Close your hood or dome over the sandwiches. Allow them to cook for 3 to 4 minutes, until the bread is golden brown. Flip and remove the sandwiches when the other sides are golden brown and the cheese has melted.

Serve while warm.

1 cup (166 g) large strawberries, chopped

4 large basil leaves, sliced thin

1 tsp extra virgin olive oil

½ tsp balsamic vinegar

¼ tsp lemon zest

Pinch of salt and ground black pepper

4 tbsp (57 g) unsalted butter

8 thin slices sourdough baguette

8 oz (226 g) Brie cheese

Griddled Chocolate-Filled Cinnamon Toast

Warning: This quick and easy dessert will have you thinking about this recipe all the time. It can be thrown together and cooked in less than 10 minutes on the Blackstone for a treat that is equal parts simple and decadent.

MAKES 4 TREATS

Set your lightly oiled griddle to medium heat. Toast your bread on each side for 1 to 2 minutes, until it starts to lightly brown.

Butter one side of each slice of warm bread. In a bowl, combine the sugar and cinnamon. Sprinkle the buttered side of the bread with a couple pinches of the cinnamon sugar mixture (you'll have some left over).

Place 4 of the buttered, sugar slices down on the medium-heat griddle. Divide the chopped chocolate up between the 4 slices and top with the remaining 4 slices, buttered side up.

Cook on each side for 2 to 3 minutes, until each side is toasty and the chocolate has melted. Remove the treats from the heat and slice diagonally.

Serve warm.

8 slices whole grain bread

4 tbsp (57 g) salted butter

1 cup (200 g) sugar

2½ tbsp (20 g) ground cinnamon

8 oz (226 g) semi-sweet or dark chocolate, chopped

Bananas Foster French Toast Grilled Cheese

Yeah, that's two different dessert grilled cheeses in the same chapter! They're that good! The combination of bananas, melty soft cheeses and crunchy bread in this recipe will have you swinging from the rafters. So, stop monkeying around and make this simple Blackstone dessert.

MAKES 4 GRILLED CHEESES

In a bowl, beat the mascarpone and cream cheese together. Set aside.

In a large, shallow bowl beat the eggs, milk and vanilla together to make the French toast batter. Stir until combined and set aside. This will help when we are dipping the bread in a moment.

Set the center of your griddle to medium heat. Once up to temp, melt 4 tablespoons (57 g) of the butter. Sprinkle the brown sugar onto the butter and stir until the sugar dissolves, 2 to 3 minutes. Add the liqueur and bring it to a simmer. Add the bananas once the mixture begins to thicken, 2 to 3 minutes. Stir until the bananas are coated, 1 to 2 minutes. Remove the bananas from the heat and allow the mixture to cool slightly. Use a squirt of water to create steam and scrape the sticky banana mixture residue from the griddle. Apply a light layer of oil back to the griddle.

Spread the mascarpone mixture evenly onto one side of each slice of bread. Top 4 slices of bread with the banana mixture on the mascarpone side. Add a sprinkle of sea salt and the remaining bread slice, cheese side down. Soak each side of each sandwich in French toast batter for about 1 minute.

On the medium-heat griddle, melt the remaining 4 tablespoons (57 g) of butter. Place each sandwich on the griddle for 3 to 4 minutes, or until the bottom is golden brown. Flip the sandwiches and cook for an additional 3 to 4 minutes, until golden brown on both sides. Remove the grilled cheeses from the griddle and allow them to rest for 2 minutes.

Serve warm.

CHEESE MIXTURE

4 oz (113 g) mascarpone cheese

4 oz (113 g) cream cheese, at room temperature

FRENCH TOAST BATTER

4 eggs

1 cup (240 ml) milk

2 tsp (10 ml) vanilla extract

BANANAS FOSTER

8 tbsp (114 g) salted butter, divided

4 tbsp (56 g) packed brown sugar

4 tbsp (60 ml) banana liqueur or brandy

2 small bananas, thickly sliced

ASSEMBLING

8 slices brioche bread

Pinch of sea salt flakes

Acknowledgments

I must thank my wife Melanie, and my kids, Makenna and Garrett, for enduring countless cold meals while I tried to get that perfect shot. Feeding you guys has been my privilege and honor. Thank you for always inspiring me to be better and calling me out to more!

A big thanks to all my friends and family who encouraged me to take on this monumental task. Never in my wildest dreams would I have ever thought something like this cookbook would be in my future.

Todd, CJ, Desirée and Nate, thank you guys so much for the introduction to the world of Blackstone! Your countless videos, livestreams, innovative cooking techniques and friendships have been amazing to watch and be a part of! Thank you all for always being so kind and welcoming me into Griddle Nation!

To Griddle Nation and specifically the Blackstone Griddle Crew, thank you all for your support, encouragement and engagement over the last several years. Leland, Michael, Ben, Vinny, Richie, Jess, Daniel, Mike, Butch, Matthew, Andy, Ryan and Steven, you guys are amazing!

To my buddy Adam McKenzie, author of *Weeknight Smoking on Your Traeger and Other Pellet Grills*, thank you for the advice and encouragement during the early stages of this process.

To the entire team at Page Street Publishing Co., thank you for the incredible experience authoring and photographing my very first, and hopefully not my last, cookbook. Thank you, Emily for walking me through each step of the process and fixing all of my Texas-inspired grammar mistakes. The design team has done an incredible job bringing this project to life and creating an amazing, finished product! I can't thank you all enough for taking a chance on this backyard cook!

A huge shout-out to my friend and mentor Matt Pittman. You, sir, are a force of nature with your dedication to this craft of outdoor cooking, yet you do it in a way that is inspiring, motivating and selfless. The way you stick your neck out for people like me is awe-inspiring, and I can't thank you enough for taking a chance on this griddle cook!

Last, but most importantly, I must thank my Lord and Savior Jesus Christ. When I found you, I was a mess, yet you loved me anyway. Thank you for constantly calling me to more and never letting me stay stagnant. You are the solid rock on which I will build my life.

About the Author

Josh Hunt is the self-taught backyard chef behind @joshhunt_griddlin. He bought his first Blackstone in April of 2020, and the rest is history! He is passionate about cooking and loves the way food brings people together. He has found a great community of home cooks, chefs and foodies on social media who all have a love for making and eating great food. Josh has had some fantastic partnerships over the years, including Blackstone, Meat Church and The Burger Smasher, to name a few. In addition, he took home the first ever Golden Spatula award in the Great Griddle Off contest hosted by Blackstone in 2020.

When Josh isn't creating and photographing recipes, he's hanging out with family, traveling to exciting new places, serving in his community and working his full-time job as a Police Detective.

Josh lives with his wife Melanie and their two children Makenna and Garrett in North Texas.

CONTACT INFO

Instagram: @joshhunt_griddlin

Facebook: @joshhuntgriddlin

Index